>> 美语 从头学

赖世雄
美语入门

> 赖世雄 著

外文出版社
FOREIGN LANGUAGES PRESS

图书在版编目(CIP)数据

美语入门 / 赖世雄著. — 北京 : 外文出版社, 2014（2019 年重印）
（美语从头学）
ISBN 978-7-119-08681-1

Ⅰ.①美… Ⅱ.①赖… Ⅲ.①英语－美国－教材 Ⅳ.①H310.1

中国版本图书馆CIP数据核字(2014)第024160号

选题策划：知语文化
特约编辑：贾志敏
责任编辑：李春英
装帧设计：郭海亭
印刷监制：冯　浩

美语入门

作　　者：赖世雄

出版发行：外文出版社有限责任公司
地　　址：北京市西城区百万庄大街24号　　邮政编码：100037
网　　址：http://www.flp.com.cn　　　　　电子邮箱：flp@cipg.org.cn
电　　话：008610-68320579（总编室）　　008610-68995964/68995883（编辑部）
　　　　　008610-68995852（发行部）　　008610-68996183（投稿电话）
印　　制：北京华创印务有限公司
经　　销：新华书店 / 外文书店
开　　本：880 mm×1230 mm　　　1/32
印　　张：8.875　　　　　　　　　　字　　数：250千字
版　　次：2019 年 1 月第 1 版第 18 次印刷
书　　号：ISBN 978-7-119-08681-1
定　　价：34.00元（平装）

序

这套《赖世雄美语从头学》系列丛书是专为英语初学者以及想重新学好英文的人士所编写的。

本系列丛书其实是我一生学习英文的缩影。1961 年,我在台北念初一起就接触英文,6 年的中学生涯中,由于语法的艰涩用语不易了解,背单词又太累,懒散的我索性放弃了学习,结果在大学联考中名落孙山,英文竟只得了 7 分(满分是 100 分)! 和很多联考失利的年轻人一样,我选择了当兵,我的英文就是在当兵期间重新学习的。这段期间我扭转了学习态度,按照自行摸索的方法,竟然让我全凭自修学好英文,后来也考上了公费赴美留学,在美国明尼苏达大学攻读大众传播及英语教学的硕士学位。可惜在念博士课程时内人罹患尿毒症,不得不中断学业,赶返台北照顾内人迄今。

从一个原本对英文一窍不通的我,到今日热爱英文并以英语教学为终身职业的我,这个转变全在于我在学习英文的路途上一路坚持。1990 年,时任中央人民广播电台科教部主任的张力先生请我在该台向全中国推广英文听、说、读、写的全向式教学。面对这项既光荣又艰巨的挑战,我随即召集台北常春藤出版社所有的中外编辑,按照我学习英文的切身经验,历经数年辛苦编写以及反复斟酌修改,这套《赖世雄美语从头学》终于问世。

为了让读者真正学懂学透这套丛书,我特别邀请发音纯正的 Jennifer 以及在台湾大学外文系任教的美籍老师 Bruce 一起逐课录制讲解。这些内容早年在中央人民广播电台播出以来就一直深受好评。阅读本套丛书时若能配合这些有声课程的使用,学习效果会远超出读者的想象。

这套丛书自从上市以来就一版再版,由此可见广大读者对这套书的信任和喜爱。这些年我们在全中国不知培养了多少因为学习本套丛书而成功的人士。例如知名的李阳老师。有一年李老师邀请我去他的广州集团总部访问时,就当面跟我说:"我就是看了您的书才有今天! "这套书上市以来,无数读者纷纷感慨相见恨晚。他们直言这套书充满了"正能量",帮助他们少走了很多弯路。一位读者通过微博告诉我们他大学四级没过,很是沮丧,经同学推荐开始学习这套书,结果一发而不可收拾,半年苦读后在研究生考试中英语取得出人意料的高分,顺利考上了研究生。还有一位同学在跟着这套教材学习之后,凭借优秀的英语能力获得了在联合国机构工作的机会。他们虽然都是普通的学子,但他们的这些进步让我们倍感欣慰。如果这套丛书能够帮助海峡两岸超过四亿的英语学习者重拾丢掉的英语,让流利的英语成为大家自信的资本,点亮以后的人生,那是一件多么荣幸的事!我本人愿以此为终身职志。

随着时代的进步,大家对英语学习资料的要求也更加多元化。我们编辑团队也在不断努力为大家提供更加便捷的学习途径,我们也在手机、网络等方面做着全新的尝试。对于本套丛书我们也一直努力改版升级。此次改版除了让版面更加赏心悦目外,重点在于我们又增加了辅助大家学习的新内容。

1. 增加了朗读音频。除了详解的讲解音频外,我们力邀美籍专业老师录制了纯正的美语朗读音频。标准的语音一定能够让你更加自信地讲英文,迅速在人群中脱颖而出。

2. 随书附赠学习手册。每册书我们都附赠一本实用手册。内含本册书的单词表、短语表以及根据读者学习程度精心设计的"对症"学习锦囊,包括生活口语、职场口语、实用写作、成语妙解等。我们希望这些锦上添花的学习资料能够将读者打造成为真正的英语全能王。

本人在人生最黄金阶段编写及讲授本套丛书,愿将它献给所有想学好英文的朋友!

学英语，其实有方法

　　由于我学英文时,听、说、读、写并重,使我多次在国际性会议中担任同声传译及在大学教学时,皆能游刃有余。我是怎么学好英语的呢? 我天赋平平,起步也就是当年的英语七分,只不过在后来的英语学习中秉持了以下三个学习态度,经历了三个学习阶段而已。

　　三个学习态度:

1. 善用零星时间:我在走路、等车、坐车、休息的时间都在说英语或看英文书籍。

2. 少就是多、慢就是快:我英文程度差,所以每天只看一两句英文,勤查字典,了解句意后,就利用零星时间慢慢地念,一遍遍地重复念,我最后竟然能够凭声音记住单词、短语或句子,不知不觉中说英语的速度也愈来愈快了。

3. 持之以恒、永不放弃:学习语言贵在勤加复习,每日不间断地练习,终有成功的一天。

　　三个学习阶段:

　　第一阶段:学习音标

　　我善用零星时间,每天只学三至四个音标,配合胶质唱片随着外籍老师灌制的录音跟着念,一遍一遍重复地念。元音学完后,再学辅音,约两个星期为一周期,如此反复练习三个月后,我打开字典就可以凭音标念出每一个英文单词的正确发音。

　　第二阶段:学习入门会话

　　我的做法是:先查字典以了解每一课会话的字词内容,再慢速将会话内容利用零星时间反复念出来。到了下午我会找个无人的地方,以一人分饰两角的方式把会话反复表演出来,并不时加入自己曾学过的词汇以扩大会话内容,如此才能活学活用。经过三个月后,我在路上见到外国人时竟然敢开口,更因为自己对发音的挑剔及自信心,常获得老外的称许。

第三阶段：大量"阅读"

我深知仅从会话学英语，所学得的词汇及常识是有限的，于是我在自修学会基础会话的能力后，便转而注重英文阅读能力的培养。

我的做法是看到文章就念出来，这才是真正的"阅读"：我选择内容生动、文字浅显的文章入门。一旦选定文章后，我本着"少就是多"的学习态度，每天只精读一小段。我会先以慢速朗读这一小段（愈慢愈好），以粗略了解这一小段的内容。再以字典勤查每一个单词，并将字典内的相关短语或例句一一抄写在笔记本上。最后，我再将该小段的英文译成中文，然后将此中文以口译的方式翻成英文。之后，就以自己的英文叙述该小段的内容，直至我当天深夜上床睡觉为止。这个做法有助于我对字词运用的了解及口译能力的培养。时至今日，我可以在阅读英文报纸或杂志之后，随即用英文说出报章杂志的内容！

读者不难发现，《赖世雄美语从头学》就是我学习英文的过程。读者购买这套丛书时，马上会发现不论哪一本书，我们都本着"完全解析"的态度将读者学习英文可能遇到的疑难杂症全都以系统而又完整的方式解说，读者在看这些书时会觉得我就在您身旁一样，不时鼓励您向前迈进。

我们都想把英文学好，我做到了，你当然也可以做到！如果你现在的程度比"七分"好，那你就可能比我做的更好。

目 录
CONTENTS

Lesson ①

Greetings
打招呼

会话 A

A: Good morning, May. How are you?

B: Hi, Tom. I'm fine. And you?

A: Not bad. Thanks.

B: Good. See you.

A: Bye.

A: 早啊，梅。你好吗？

B: 嗨，汤姆。我很好，你呢？

A: 还不错，谢了。

B: 很好，再见。

A: 再见。

会话 B

A: Hi, May. How's it going?

B: Great. And how are you doing?

A: Not bad.

B: OK. See you later.

A: Take care.

B: You, too.

A: 嗨，梅。近来如何？

B: 很好。那你呢？

A: 还不错。

B: 好吧，再见。

A: 保重。

B: 你也是。

2 **Vocabulary & Idioms** 单词短语注解

会话 A

1. **good morning** 早上好
   good [gʊd] 形 好的；morning [ˈmɔrnɪŋ] 名 早晨

2. **May** [me] 名 梅（女性名）

3. **How are you?** 你好吗？
   how [haʊ] 副 如何；are [ɑr] 动 是（与 you, they 等表"你、你们、他们"连用）；you [ju] 代 你（们）

4. **Tom** [tɑm] 名 汤姆（男性名）

5. **hi** [haɪ] 叹 嗨（打招呼用语）

6. **I'm fine.**（是"I am fine."的缩写）我很好。
   I [aɪ] 代 我；am [æm] 动 是（与 I 连用）；fine [faɪn] 形 不错的

7. **And you?**（此处是"And how are you?"的简化）那你呢？
   and [ænd] 连 那么

8. **Not bad.** 还不错。
   not [nɑt] 副 不；bad [bæd] 形 坏的

9. **thanks** [θæŋks] 名 谢谢

10. **See you.** 再见。
    see [si] 动 看见

11. **bye** [baɪ] 叹 再见（是 goodbye [gʊdˈbaɪ] 的简化）

会话 B

1. **How's it going?**（是"How is it going?"的缩写）近况如何？
   is [ɪz] 动 是（与 it, she, he 等表"它、她、他"连用）
   it [ɪt] 代 它（此指"生活"）
   going [ˈgoɪŋ] 动 发展；走（由 go 变化而成）

2. **great** [gret] 形 很棒的

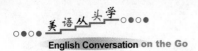

3. **And how are you doing?** 那么你好吗?（此处即等于"And you?"）
   doing ['duɪŋ] 动 表现（由 do 变化而成）

4. **OK** [ˌo'ke] 形 不错的

5. **See you later.** 再见。(= See you.)
   later ['letɚ] 副 稍后, 以后

6. **Take care.** 保重。
   take [tek] 动 拿, 取; care [kɛr] 名 谨慎

7. **You, too.** 你也一样（此处是"You take care, too."的简化形式）
   too [tu] 副 也

3 *Grammar Points* 语法重点 ≈

会话 A

1. **good morning** 早上好
   本用语是表示礼貌的招呼语, 用于中午 12 点以前。
   其他相同的招呼语如下:
   Good afternoon. 下午好。（见面时使用）
   Good evening. 晚上好。（见面时使用）
   Good night. 晚安。（道别时使用, 相当于 goodbye 之意）

2. 与人道别时, 表"再见"的常用语如下:
   Goodbye. 再见。（正式）
   Bye. 再见。（非正式, 与熟识的朋友使用）
   See you later. 再见 / 待会儿见。
   = See you.
   See you tomorrow. 明天见。

3. 有些美国年轻人喜欢使用下列俏皮的对话:
   A: See you later. 再见。
   B: Alligator. 鳄鱼。
   此处 B 故意说"Alligator."取代"See you later."乃因 alligator
   ['æləˌgetɚ] 中的 gator 与"See you later."中的 later 押韵。

alligator 原指"鳄鱼"，此处全无任何意义，纯属俏皮话，视为"See you later."之意。

4. 注意下列问候语的区别：

How are you? 你好吗？（多用于正式场合）

* How are you doing? 你好吗？（多用于熟识朋友之间）

How are you getting along? 你好吗？

How have you been? 你最近还好吗 / 近况如何？

* How's it going? 还好吧 / 近况如何？

* What's up? 近况如何？（多为年轻人所使用）

What's happening? 近况如何？（= What's up?）

有 * 符号者乃为最常用问候语。

5. 注意下列的答句：

a. 上列问候语中，前三个问句均有 you，故可使用下列答句：

问句： How are you? 你好吗？

= How are you doing?

= How are you getting along?

答句： I'm fine, thank you. 我很好，谢谢你。

Great, thanks. 很好，谢谢你。

Fine, thanks. 不错，谢谢你。

Not bad, thanks. 还不错，谢谢你。

So-so, thank you. 马马虎虎 / 还过得去，谢谢你。

b. "How have you been?"是"How are you?"的完成时，故答句不可说"I'm fine, thank you."或"I am fine, thank you.",而要说"I have been fine, thank you."或"Fine, thank you."。

c. 问候句"How's it going?"、"What's up?"及"What's happening?"分别为"How is it going?"、"What is up?"及"What is happening?"的缩写形式。唯实际使用时，应使用缩写形式。

上述问候句的主语并非 you，故答句不可说"I'm fine, thank you.",现分述如下：

问句： How's it going? 近况如何？

答句： Not bad, thank you. 还不错，谢谢你。

So-so, thank you. 马马虎虎，谢谢你。

Great, thank you. 很好，谢谢你。

Fine, thank you. 不错，谢谢你。

问句： What's up?/What's happening? 近况如何？

答句： Nothing much. 没什么。

Same as usual. 老样子。

* "Same as usual." 由 "Everything is the same as usual."（一切与往常相同。）简化而来。

same [sem] 形 相同的; as [æz] 连 和

usual [ˈjuʒʊəl] 形 平常的

6. 表"感谢"的用语：

Thanks. 谢谢。（在非正式的场合或朋友之间广为使用，此处 Thanks 是复数的名词）

Thank you. 谢谢你。（较正式）

Thank you very much. 非常谢谢你。（最正式）

Thanks a lot. 多谢。（非正式）

Thanks a million. 很谢谢你。（谢谢你一百万次。俏皮用语）

会话 B

1. **OK.** 好。

本用语相当于 "All right." 之意。

例 A: Let's go. 咱们走吧！

B: All right. 好。

2. **Take care.** 保重。

本句系由 "I hope you will take care of yourself."（我希望你会照顾自己。）简化而成。

take care of... 照顾……

例 Don't worry. I will take care of you. 别担心，我会照顾你。

3. **You, too.** 你也一样。

这是一种简答句，系由下列句子简化而成：

I hope you will take care of yourself, too. 我希望你也能照顾你自己。

注意

这种简答句只用于肯定句中，且通常只有下列两种：

You, too. 你 / 你们也一样。

Me, too. 我也一样。

例 A: I hope you can pass the exam. 我希望你考试能及格。

B: You, too. 你也一样。

= I hope you can pass the exam, too.

A: I hope I can see you tomorrow. 我希望明天能见到你。

B: Me, too. 我也一样。

= I hope I can see you tomorrow, too.

4 Substitution 替换

1. Good | morning,
         | afternoon, May. 早上好 / 中午好 / 晚上好，梅。
         | evening,

2. How are | you?
            | you doing? 你好吗？

3. I'm | fine.
        | OK. 我很好 / 还好。

4. And
   What about | you? 那你呢？
   How about

5. Not bad.
   Great. | Thanks. 还不错 / 很好 / 还好，谢了。
   Fine.

6. | Thanks. 谢谢。
   | Thank you. 谢谢你。
   | Thank you very much. 非常谢谢你。
   | Thanks a lot. 多谢。

7. Good. | See you.
       | See you later.
       | Bye.   很好，再见。
       | Goodbye

8. | How's it going?
   | What's up?   近来如何？
   | What's happening?

5 Exercises 练习 ☾

1. Use the right word: 请选出适当的单词：

See	Good	Same	much
Not	going	What's	How

1. _See_ you later.
2. How's it _going_?
3. _What's_ happening?
4. _Not_ bad, thanks.
5. _Good_ evening.
6. _How_ are you?
7. Nothing _much_.
8. _Same_ as usual.

2. Complete the dialogue: 完成下列会话：

Sam: Hi, Sally. How are you?
Sally: _Not_ b_ad_. And you?
Sam: Great! And how is Bob?
Sally: He's f_ine_.
Sam: Good.
Sally: See you later.
Sam: T_ake_ c_are_.
Sally: You too.

Lesson ②

Courtesy
礼貌

会话 A

A: Excuse me. Are you Ann?

B: No. I'm not.

A: Oh, I'm sorry. Who's Ann?

B: She is.

A: Thank you.

B: You're welcome.

A: 对不起，请问你是安吗？

B: 不，我不是。

A: 喔，很抱歉。请问谁是安？

B: 她是。

A: 谢谢。

B: 不客气。

会话 B

A: Hi, I'm Tom.

B: I beg your pardon?

A: I'm Tom.

B: Oh! Hi, Tom. I'm May.

A: Nice to meet you, May.

B: Pleased to meet you.

A: 嗨，我是汤姆。

B: 对不起，请再说一遍好吗？

A: 我是汤姆。

B: 哦！嗨，汤姆。我是梅。

A: 很高兴认识你，梅。

B: 幸会，幸会。

idiot = pumpkin-head

2 *Vocabulary & Idioms* 单词短语注解 ✎

会话 A

1. **courtesy** [ˈkɜtəsɪ] 名 礼貌

2. **Excuse me.** 对不起 / 打扰一下。
   excuse [ɪkˈskjuz] 动 原谅，宽恕

3. **Ann** [æn] 名 安（女性名）

4. **no** [no] 副 不是

5. **I'm sorry.**（是 "I am sorry." 的缩写）对不起 / 抱歉。
   sorry [ˈsɔrɪ] 形 抱歉的

6. **who** [hu] 疑 谁（本文 who's 是 who is 的缩写）

7. **Thank you.** 谢谢你。
   thank [θæŋk] 动 感谢，向……致谢

8. **You're welcome.** 不客气 / 不用谢。
   （是 "You are welcome." 的缩写）
   welcome [ˈwɛlkəm] 形 不客气的，受欢迎的

会话 B

1. **I beg your pardon?** 对不起，请再说一遍好吗？
   beg [bɛg] 动 请求，恳求；pardon [ˈpɑrdn̩] 名 原谅，宽恕

2. **oh** [o] 叹 哦，啊

3. **Nice to meet you.** 很高兴认识你 / 幸会。
   nice [naɪs] 形 好的，令人愉快的；meet [mit] 动 与……会面 / 认识

4. **Pleased to meet you.** 很高兴认识你 / 幸会。
   pleased [plizd] 形 高兴的，乐意的

3 *Grammar Points* 语法重点 〜〜

会话 A

1. **Excuse me.** 对不起 / 打扰一下。

   I'm sorry. 对不起 / 抱歉。

   以上两句均译成"对不起",但用法有别 :

   "Excuse me."用于唤起别人的注意 ; 而 "I'm sorry." 则多表"抱歉",尤其是在犯错或有不好的消息要告诉对方时使用。

   例 A: Excuse me. Where is the station?

   　　B: I'm sorry. I'm new here.

   　　A: 对不起 / 打扰一下,车站在哪儿?

   　　B: 抱歉,我刚到这儿 / 我在这儿人生地不熟。

   　　I'm sorry. I can't see you today. 抱歉,我今天无法见你。

   注意

   "Excuse me." 或 "I'm sorry." 之后除可置句号以外,亦可置逗号,再置连词 but,以连接另一个句子。but 原意为"但是",但此处不必译出。因此上列例句亦可写成 :

   Excuse me, but where is the station?

   I'm sorry, but I'm new here.

   I'm sorry, but I can't see you today.

2. **You're welcome.** 别客气。

   对方表示谢谢时,可用下列句子或用语回答,这些句子或用语均译成"别客气"。

   例 A: Thank you for your help. 谢谢你的帮忙。

   　　B: You're welcome. 别客气。

   　　　Don't mention it.

   　　　Not at all.

   　　　No problem.

会话 B

1. **I beg your pardon?** 对不起,请再说一遍好吗?
   本问句理应说成:
   May I beg your pardon? 我可以请求你的原谅吗?
   但因为经常使用的关系,反而简化成如下用语:
   I beg your pardon?
   = Beg your pardon?
   = Pardon me?
   = Pardon?
   以上问句均译成"对不起,请再说一遍好吗?",这是很客气的用语。

2. **Nice to meet you.** 很高兴认识你 / 幸会。
   = Pleased to meet you.
   = Glad to meet you.
   以上三句均表"幸会",是两人初见面时的客气用语。这三句分别由下列完整的句子简化而成:
   It's nice to meet you. 认识你真好。
   I'm pleased to meet you. 我很高兴认识你。
   I'm glad to meet you. 我很高兴认识你。

3. 英文中很多句子都是"代词 **+ be** 动词"开头的,如下:
   I am a boy. 我是男孩。
   It is a book. 那是书。
   You are very kind. 你心肠真好。
   但在口语中,常为求说话的速度及口气的自然,经常将"代词 + be 动词"简化,而形成下列的形态:
   I'm a boy.
   It's a book.
   You're very kind.
   现列表如下:

"代词＋be 动词" 简化表			
人称		简化前	简化后
第一人称	单数	I am 我是	I'm [aɪm]
	复数	we are 我们是	we're [wɪr]
第二人称	单数	you are 你是	you're [jur]
	复数	you are 你们是	you're [jur]
第三人称	单数	he is 他是	he's [hiz]
		she is 她是	she's [ʃiz]
		it is 它是	it's [ɪts]
	复数	they are 他／她／它们是	they're [ðer]

试将下列含 "代词＋be 动词" 的句型简化：

1. They are my good friends. 他们是我的好友。

2. He is my father. 他是我爸爸。

3. You are very nice. 你人很好。

4. We are hungry now. 我们现在肚子饿了。

5. It is a cute dog. 它是只很可爱的狗。

解答：

1. They're my good friends.

2. He's my father.

3. You're very nice.

4. We're hungry now.

5. It's a cute dog.

4 *Substitution* 替换

1. You're welcome.
   Don't mention it.　不客气。
   Not at all.
   No problem.

2. I beg your pardon?
   Beg your pardon?　对不起，请再说一遍好吗？
   Pardon me?
   Pardon?

3. Nice
   Pleased ｜to meet you. 很高兴认识你 / 幸会。
   Glad

4. I'm Tom. 我是汤姆。
   She's May. 她是梅。
   They're students. 他 / 她们是学生。

5 *Exercises* 练习

I. Use the right word: 请选出适当的单词：

| meet | all | Excuse | beg |
| problem | but | mention | Where |

1. _Excuse_ me.
2. I'm sorry, _but_ I can't see you today.
3. I _beg_ your pardon?
4. Don't _mention_ it.
5. Not at _all_ .
6. Nice to _meet_ you.
7. No _problem_ .
8. _Where_ is the station?

II. Complete the dialogue: 完成下列会话：

Tom: Excuse m e   . Are you Sue?

May: No. I'm n ot .

Tom: Oh! I'm sorry, b wt   is she Sue?

May: Yes, s he   is.

Tom: Great. Thanks a l ot .

May: You're w el come

Tom: Bye!

Lesson 3

Name, Age and Nationality

姓名、年龄和国籍

1 *Dialogue* 会话

会话 A

A: Excuse me. What's your name?

B: I'm May.

A: Hi, May. Where are you from?

B: I'm from Hong Kong. What about you?

A: I'm from Japan.

A: 对不起。请问你叫什么名字？

B: 我叫梅。

A: 嗨，梅。你是哪里人呢？

B: 我是香港人。那你呢？

A: 我是日本人。

会话 B

A: May I have your name, please?

B: My name is May.

A: How old are you?

B: I'm twenty-five.

A: Where are you from?

B: I'm from Hong Kong.

A: 请问尊姓大名？

B: 我叫梅。

A: 你几岁了？

B: 我 25 岁。

A: 你是哪里人？

B: 我是香港人。

2 *Vocabulary & Idioms* 单词短语注解

会话 A

1. **name** [nem] 名姓名，名字

2. **age** [edʒ] 名年龄

3. **nationality** [ˌnæʃəˈnælətɪ] 名国籍

4. **What's your name?** 你叫什么名字？
   what [hwɑt] 疑什么

5. **Where are you from?** 你是哪里人？
   where [hwɛr] 副何处；from [frɑm] 介由（何处），从……

6. **Hong Kong** [ˈhɑŋˈkɑŋ] 名香港（地名）

7. **What about you?** 那你呢？(= How about you?)
   about [əˈbaʊt] 介关于

8. **Japan** [dʒəˈpæn] 名日本（国名）

会话 B

1. **May I have your name, please?** 请问尊姓大名？
   may [me] 助可以
   have [hæv] 动有
   please [pliz] 副请（一种有礼貌的请求用语）

2. **How old are you?** 你几岁了？
   old [old] 形老的

3. **twenty-five** [ˌtwɛntɪˈfaɪv] 名25
   twenty [ˈtwɛntɪ] 名20；five [faɪv] 名5

3 *Grammar Points* 语法重点 ⋘

会话 A

1. 疑问句造句法：

本段会话中，"What's your name?" 以及 "Where are you from?" 为含有疑问词 what（什么）及 where（什么地方）的问句，称为特殊疑问句。

a. 形成此类特殊问句的疑问词常用的有：what（什么，何物）、which（哪一个）、who（谁）、where（何地）、when（何时）、how（如何）等，在问句中，这些疑问词一定放在句首。

   例 Who is Mary? 玛丽是谁？

   What can he do? 他能做什么？

b. 中文疑问句与英文疑问句的结构通常是不相同的。中文的疑问句与陈述句结构完全相同，只是前者在句尾加上问号，而后者则置句号。

   例 疑问句：他是谁？

   陈述句：他是彼得。

   疑问句：你籍贯哪儿？

   陈述句：我籍贯河南。

c. 但在英文句型中，疑问句及陈述句则有明显的区别。

   例 疑问句：Who is he?

   陈述句：He is Peter.

   疑问句：Where are you from?

   陈述句：I'm from Henan.

d. 由于中英文结构不尽相同，常造成英文初学者的困扰，因此下列的解说一定要熟记，并多多练习造句，方能习惯这些结构。

   （1）先按中文习惯造一个含疑问词的句子：

他是谁？	→	He is who?
他何时会来？	→	He when will come?
他住在哪里？	→	He lives where?

   （2）再将疑问词置于句首，即：

He is who?　　　　　→ <u>Who</u> he is?

He when will come? → <u>When</u> he will come?

He lives where?　　 → <u>Where</u> he lives?

（3）若主语之后有 be 动词时，be 动词与主语要倒装，即：

Who <u>he is</u>? →　Who <u>is he</u>? （√）

* be 动词就是表"是"的动词，如：is、am、are 等。

（4）若主语之后有助动词时，助动词与主语要倒装，即：

When <u>he will</u> come? → When <u>will he</u> come?

* 助动词就是置于动词之前，用以帮助该动词加强其意思或语气的一种词类。常用的助动词有 will（将会）、can（能够）、may（也许）等。

（5）若主语之后只有动词时，则要在主语前置另一种助动词 do 或 does，且原来的动词要变成原形，即：

Where <u>he lives</u>? →　Where <u>does</u> he <u>live</u>?

不可写成：

Where <u>lives</u> he?（×）

* 此处的 do 或 does 是帮助我们问问题的助动词。does 要与第三人称单数的主语（如 he、she、it、Mary、Tom、a boy 等）连用。原句"Where he lives?"中，he 是第三人称单数，故应使用 does，即成"Where does he live?"的正确说法。

do 则可与第三人称单数的主语以外的任何主语连用。

第三人称复数主语：

Where <u>do</u> May and Tom live? 梅和汤姆住在哪里？

When <u>do</u> they go to school? 他们何时上学？

第二人称单复数主语：

What <u>do</u> you like? 你 / 你们喜欢什么？

第一人称单复数主语：

What <u>do</u> I need? 我需要什么？

When <u>do</u> we go? 我们何时走？

e.　疑问词 who（谁）、what（什么，何物）及 which（哪一个）是疑问代词，可作主语，此时形成的问句句型与中文问句完全一样，故不采用倒装句型。

例 中文：谁会来？

英文：Who will come?（非 Will who come?）

中文：哪一个比较好？

英文：Which is better?（非 Is which better?）←Witch

2. 表示"您是哪里人 / 籍贯哪里 ？"有下列说法：

Where are you from? 您是哪里人 ？

= Where do you come from?

What's your nationality? 您是什么国籍 ？

以上三个问句中，前两句可用以询问对方的省籍或国籍，但最后一句则仅限于国籍。请看下列对话：

A: Where are you from? 您是哪里人 ？

 = Where do you come from?

B: I'm from New York. / I'm from America.

= I come from New York. / I come from America.

我是纽约人。/ 我是美国人。

A: What's your nationality? 您是哪国人 ？

B: I'm Japanese. 我是日本人。= I'm a Japanese
n.

3. **What about you?** 那你呢 ？(adj.)

= How about you?

这是一种简化的问句，以省略重复的单词或短语。这种句型在会话中常见，极为实用。请看下列句子的比较：

I love music. Do you love music, too?（可）

我喜欢音乐。你也喜欢音乐吗 ？

→ I love music. What about you?（佳）

= I love music. How about you?

He is from China. Where is she from?（可）他是中国人。那她呢 ？

→ He is from China. What about her?（佳）

= He is from China. How about her?

会话 B

1. **May I have your name, please?** 请问尊姓大名？

   = May I know your name, please?

   What's your name? 你叫什么名字？

   a. 上列两个问句均是向对方请教姓名的问句。虽然意思相同，但显然第一个问句语气较客气有礼，多在正式的场合中使用。第二个问句则为长辈对晚辈或上司对下属使用。

   b. please 的使用时机：

   这是个副词，多置于句尾，之前置逗号，可用以减缓命令的口气。

   例 Come here. 过来。——不客气

   → Come here, please. 请过来。

   = Please come here.

   c. 我们若想做某事而欲征求对方的同意时，可使用下列句型：

   May I..., please? 请问我可以……吗？

   例 May I open the window? （可）我可以打开窗户吗？

   → May I open the window, please? （更客气）

   请问我可以打开窗户吗？

2. **How old are you?** 你几岁了？

   = What's your age? 你年龄多大？

   以上都是询问对方年龄的问句。咱们中国人彼此见面可以询问对方年龄，但与西方人交往时，除非对方主动透露自己的年龄，否则我们随意询问别人的年龄会被视为不礼貌的行为。

④ Substitution 替换

1. What's | your / his / her | name? 你 / 他 / 她叫什么名字？

2. I'm / My name's | May. 我叫 / 我的名字是梅。

3.　Where │are you from?　你是哪里人?
　　　　　 │do you come from?

4.　I │am │from Hong Kong. 我是香港人。
　　 │come

5.　May I │have │your name, please? 请问尊姓大名?
　　　　　 │know

6.　How old │are you?
　　　　　　 │is he?　你 / 他 / 她几岁了?
　　　　　　 │is she?

7.　I'm │twenty-five.
　　　　 │twenty-five years old.　我 25 岁。

8.　I'm │Japanese.
　　　　│Chinese.　我是日本人 / 中国人 / 美国人。
　　　　│American.

5　Exercises 练习　☪

I.　Use the right word: 请选出适当的单词:

will	May	How	old
come	does	What's	Where

1.　__How__ old are you?

2.　__What's__ your name?

3.　I'm forty years __old__.

4.　__Where__ are you from?

5.　__May__ I have your name?

6.　Where __does__ she live?

7.　When __will__ you come?

8.　Where do you __come__ from?

II.　Complete the dialogue: 完成下列会话:

Tom:　Excuse me. What's y__our__ name, please?

May: I'm May.

Tom: Hi, May. Where a _re_ you from?

May: I'm from Japan. H_ow_ about you?

Tom: I c_ome_ from America. I'm A_merica_

May: I beg your _pardon_?

Tom: I'm from America.

May: Oh, I see.

Lesson 4

Introductions
介绍

1 *Dialogue* 会话

会话 A

A: Hi, Tom! How's it going?

B: Great! Who's your friend?

A: Oh! I'm sorry. This is Kay.

B: Pleased to meet you, Kay.

C: Nice to meet you.

A: 嗨，汤姆！近来如何？

B: 很好！你的朋友怎么称呼？

A: 噢！真抱歉。这位是凯。

B: 幸会，凯。

C: 幸会。

会话 B

A: Dad. Please meet my girlfriend, May.

B: Glad to meet you, May.

C: Glad to meet you, too, Mr. Lin.

B: And what is your family name, May?

C: It's Chen. But you may call me May.

B: May Chen. It's a nice name.

C: Thank you, sir.

A: 爸爸，见见我的女朋友梅。

B: 很高兴认识你，梅。

C: 我也很高兴认识您，林先生。

B: 梅，那么你贵姓呀？

C: 我姓陈。不过您可以叫我梅。

B: 陈梅，这是个好名字。

C: 谢谢您，先生。

2 *Vocabulary & Idioms* 单词短语注解

会话 A

1. **introduction** [ˌɪntrəˈdʌkʃən] 名 介绍，引见

2. **friend** [frɛnd] 名 朋友

3. **this** [ðɪs] 代 这个

4. **Kay** [ke] 名 凯 (女性名)

会话 B

1. **dad** [dæd] 名 爸爸 (比 father [ˈfɑðə] 更亲昵的称呼)

2. **girlfriend** [ˈɡɝlˌfrɛnd] 名 女朋友

3. **glad** [ɡlæd] 形 高兴的

4. **Mr. Lin** 林先生
   Mr. [ˈmɪstə] 名 先生 (称呼语，是 Mister 的缩写形式)
   Lin [lɪn] 名 林 (姓氏)

5. **family name** 姓 (= last name = surname [ˈsɝˌnem])
   family [ˈfæməlɪ] 形 家族／庭的 & 名 家族／庭

6. **Chen** [tʃɛn] 名 陈 (姓氏)

7. **but** [bʌt] 连 但是

8. **call** [kɔl] 动 叫，称

9. **sir** [sɝ] 名 先生 (称呼语)

3 *Grammar Points* 语法重点

会话 A

1. 将熟识的人介绍给对方时，一般而言，有一个遵循的法则：
   男性被介绍给女性或晚辈被介绍给长辈，以示礼貌。
   请看下列会话：

John:　Mary, this is Jack.

Mary:　Hi, Jack. Glad to meet you.

Jack:　Glad to meet you, too.

约翰：玛丽，这位是杰克。

玛丽：嗨，杰克。幸会。

杰克：幸会。

Son:　Dad, this is May.

Dad:　Pleased to meet you, May.

May:　Glad to meet you, too, Mr. Wilson.

儿子：爸，这位是梅。

爸爸：梅，很高兴认识你。

梅：威尔逊先生，我也很高兴认识您。

2. **This is Kay.** 这位是凯。

此处 This 是指示代词，表"这个"。

指示代词就是指名某个或某些东西的代词，通常有四个：
this（这个）、that（那个）、these（这些）、those（那些）。前两者代替单数的名词，后两者则代替复数的名词。

通常离说话者较近的东西，应使用 this 或 these 代替，而离说话者较远的东西，则使用 that 或 those 代替，参阅下列图示：

例 A: What is that? 那是什么？

　B: That is a dog. 那是狗。

　A: What are those? 那些是什么？

　B: Those are books. 那些是书。

A: What is this? 这是什么?

B: This is a pen. 这是笔。

A: What are these? 这些是什么?

B: These are my toys. 这些是我的玩具。

注意

a. 在答句时, 为了避免与指示代词重复, 可用 it (它) 代替 this 或 that, they (它们) 代替 these 或 those。

故上列各答句均可改为:

It is a dog.

They are books.

It is a pen.

They are my toys.

b. this / that / these / those 除可作指示代词外, 亦可有形容词的功能, 之后接名词, 此时 this / that / these / those 就称为指示形容词。

例 This is a good book. 这是本好书。

指示代词

This book is good. 这本书很好。

指示形容词

That is a chair. 那是椅子。

指示代词

That chair is red. 那把椅子是红色的。

指示形容词

会话 B

1. <u>And what is your family name, May?</u> 梅, 那么你贵姓呀?

   a. 此处句首的 And 是语气词, 可译成"那么"、"呃"。不过 and 通常作连词用, 译成"和"、"与"之意。

      例 He and I are good friends. 他和我是好朋友。

   b. 中文的"姓名", 在英文中有下列说法:

      姓: family name

      = last name

      = surname

      名: first name

      = given name

      例 A: May I have your name, please? 请问尊姓大名?

      B: My family name is Zhang, and my given name is Li-pei. But you can call me Peter.

      = Zhang is my last name, and Li-pei is my first name. But you can call me Peter.

      我姓张, 名立培, 不过你可以叫我彼得。

2. **Glad to meet you, too, Mr. Lin.** 我也很高兴认识您, 林先生。

   下列是常用的礼貌称谓语:

   Mr. Wang 王先生(Mr. 是 Mister [ˈmɪstə] 的缩写形式)

   Mrs. Wang 王太太(Mrs. 是 Missus / Missis [ˈmɪsɪz] 的缩写形式)

   Miss Wang 王小姐(Miss [mɪs] 多置于未婚女士的姓氏前)

   Ms. Wang 王女士(Ms. [mɪz] 置于已婚或未婚女士的姓氏前)

   注意

   我们见到某女士, 知其未婚时, 就用 Miss 称呼, 但无法确知其已婚或未婚时, 则用 Ms. 称呼。

   例 Mr. & Mrs. Wang are English teachers. They have a daughter. We call her Miss Wang. She has a friend. She is Ms. Lin. Miss Wang and Ms. Lin are very good friends.

   王氏夫妇是英文老师, 他们有一个女儿, 我们称呼她王小姐。她有一位朋友, 她是林女士。王小姐和林女士是很要好的朋友。

4 Substitution 替换

1. This | is Kay. 这位 / 她是凯。
    She

2. What's your | family name? | 你贵姓?
    last name?
    surname?

3. Glad to meet you, | Mr. Lin. 我也很高兴认识你,林先生。
    too, | Mrs. Wang. 我也很高兴认识你,王太太。
    | Miss Lin. 我也很高兴认识你,林小姐。
    | Ms. Chen. 我也很高兴认识你,陈女士。

4. This | is a book. 这 / 那是一本书。
    That

5. These | are my students. 这些 / 那些是我的学生。
    Those

6. This | pen is red. 这 / 那支笔是红色的。
    That

7. These | chairs are green. 这些 / 那些椅子是绿色的。
    Those

5 Exercises 练习

I. Use the right word: 请选出适当的单词:

Who's	meet	This	call
These	It's	to	family

1. Please _meet_ my mother, Jane.

2. _This_ is my girlfriend, Tina.

3. Glad _to_ meet you.

4. _It's_ a nice name.

5. You may _call_ me Bob.

6. What's your _family_ name?

32

7. _Who's_ your friend?

8. _Those_ are my books.

II. Complete the dialogue: 完成下列会话：

Tom: Hi, May!

May: Hi, Tom! How's it g_oing_ ?

Tom: Not b_ad_ .

May: W_ho's_ your friend?

Tom: Oh! I'm sorry. T_his_ is Rob. He's m_y_ brother.

May: Hi, Rob! I'm May.

Rob: G_lad_ to meet you, May.

May: P_leased_ to meet you, Rob.

Lesson 5

Occupations

職業

会话 A

A: Excuse me, Mr. Li. This is Miss Lin.

B: How do you do, Miss Lin?

C: How do you do?

A: Miss Lin works for IBM.

B: What a coincidence! I work in a computer company, too.

A: 打扰一下，李先生。这位是林小姐。

B: 林小姐，你好！

C: 你好！

A: 林小姐在 IBM 公司上班。

B: 好巧呀！我也是在一家计算机公司上班。

会话 B

A: Hi, Tom! I'd like you to meet my friend, Sal.

B: Pleased to meet you, Sal.

C: Same here.

B: So, what do you do, Sal?

C: I'm a secretary. What about you?

B: I'm a pilot.

A: 嗨，汤姆。我想请你见见我的朋友莎儿。

B: 很高兴认识你，莎儿。

C: 我也一样。

B: 那，你从事哪一行的?

C: 我是个秘书。你呢?

B: 我是飞行员。

② ***Vocabulary & Idioms*** 单词短语注解 ✍

会话 A

1. **occupation** [ˌɑkjəˈpeʃən] 名 职业

2. **How do you do?** 你好！（初次见面时的礼貌用语）

3. **work for...** 为……工作；work [wɝk] 动 工作

4. **What a coincidence!** 好巧呀！
   coincidence [koˈɪnsədəns] 名 巧合

5. **work in** 在……上班

6. **computer** [kəmˈpjutɚ] 名 计算机

7. **company** [ˈkʌmpənɪ] 名 公司

会话 B

1. **I'd like you to...** （是 "I would like you to..." 的缩写）
   would [wʊd] 助 表示请求、希望的一种助动词
   like [laɪk] 动 想，希望（与 would 连用）

2. **Sal** [sæl] 名 莎儿（女性名）

3. **Same here!** 我也一样！
   same [sem] 形 相同的；here [hɪr] 副（在）这里

4. **What do you do?** 你从事哪一行的？

5. **secretary** [ˈsɛkrəˌtɛrɪ] 名 秘书

6. **pilot** [ˈpaɪlət] 名 飞行员，驾驶员

③ ***Grammar Points*** 语法重点 〰

会话 A

1. **How do you do, Miss Lin?** 林小姐，你好！
   a. "How do you do?" 是两人第一次见面时，表示礼貌的用语。虽

是问句，但实则等于中文的"你 / 您好！"，对方听到这句话时，亦以同样的话回应。即：

Miss Lin : How do you do, Mr. Wang? 林小姐：王先生，你好！

Mr. Wang: How do you do, Miss Lin? 王先生：林小姐，你好！

b. 比较 "How do you do?" 与 "How are you?" 及 "How're you doing?" 的不同：

前句相当中文的"你 / 您好！"，不要译成："你 / 您好吗？"，故不可以 "I'm fine, thank you."（我很好，谢谢你 / 您。）回应。即：

例 A: How do you do?

B: I'm fine, thank you. (×)

→ How do you do? (√)

而 "How are you?" 或 "How're you doing?" 则是一种使用于认识的朋友之间，纯粹表示关怀对方身体的问候语，故可用 "I'm fine, thank you." 回应。

例 A: How're you doing?

B: Fine, thank you. (√)

2. **work for...** 为……工作

例 He works for a travel agency. 他替某旅行社工作。

比较：

He works in a travel agency. 他在某旅行社上班。

＊以上两句意思相同，均可译成"他任职于某旅行社。"

3. **What a coincidence!** 好巧呀！

本句是已简化过的感叹句。原句完整的写法为：

What a coincidence this / it is! 这真是个巧合呀！

感叹句一共有两种，一为 what 引导，另一为 how 引导，what 与 how 均译成"多么的"或"好（个）……"，造句法则如下：

a. 以 what 引导的感叹句句型如下：

What ＋ 名词 ＋ 主语 ＋ be 动词！ 好（个）……呀！

（1）先造一个含有"主语 ＋ be 动词 ＋ 名词"结构的句子，即：

This is a good movie. 这是部好电影。

John is a filial son. 约翰是个孝顺的儿子。

Mary and John are good students. 玛丽和约翰是好学生。

（2）再于句首冠以 what，并将名词置于 what 之后，句尾置感叹号，便大功告成，即：

What a good movie this is! 这真是部好电影呀！

What a filial son John is! 约翰真是个孝顺的儿子呀！

What good students Mary and John are!

玛丽和约翰是多么好的学生呀！

（3）实际使用时，通常将"主语＋be 动词"予以省略，而采用下列简化的说法：

What a good movie! 好棒的电影呀！

What a filial son! 好孝顺的儿子呀！

What good students! 多么好的学生呀！

b. 以 how 引导的感叹句句型如下：

How＋形容词＋主语＋be 动词！ 多么……呀！

（1）先造一个含有"主语＋be 动词＋形容词"结构的句子，即：

John is nice. 约翰不错。

She is beautiful. 她很美。

The children are diligent. 这些孩子很用功。

（2）再于句首冠以 how，并将形容词置于 how 之后，句尾置感叹号，便完成了，即：

How nice John is! 约翰好棒呀！

How beautiful she is! 她多美呀！

How diligent the children are! 这些孩子多么用功呀！

（3）一如 what 引导的感叹句，在实际使用时，how 引导的感叹句中，"主语＋be 动词"常予以省略，而采用下列简化的说法：

How nice! 多棒呀！

How beautiful! 多美呀！

How diligent! 多用功呀！

会话 B

1. **I'd like you to meet my friend, Sal.**
我想请你见见我的朋友，莎儿。

本句型"I'd like..."由"I would like..."简化而成，是一种请求某人做某事，但语气客气的祈使句。句型如下：

I'd like＋人＋to＋动词原形　我想请某人从事……

例 I'd like you to meet my sister. 我想请你见见我妹妹。

I'd like you to sing a song. 我想请你唱首歌。

I'd like Peter to write a letter for me. 我想请彼得替我写一封信。

注意

若表"我想要……"时，则可采用下列句型：

I'd like to＋动词原形　我想要……

例 I'd like to sing a song for you. 我想要为诸位唱首歌。

比较：I like to sing. 我喜欢唱歌。

2. **Tom: Pleased to meet you, Sal.**（汤姆）很高兴认识你，莎儿。

Sal: Same here.（莎儿）我也一样。

此处"Same here."按字义译成"这里是相同的"。实则译成"我也一样"。相当于"Me, too."（我也一样。），此处则等于"Pleased to meet you, too."（我也很高兴认识你。）；换言之，"Same here."或"Me, too."可用来表示赞同对方的意见。

例 A: I love music. 我喜欢音乐。

B: Same here./Me, too. 我也一样。

* 此处的"Same here."等于"I love music, too."我也喜欢音乐。

3. **What do you do?** 你从事哪一行的？

＝ What's your occupation? 你的职业是什么？

＝ What's your job? 你的工作是什么？

在"What do you do?"的问句中，第一个do是助动词，本身不具任何意义，故不须翻译，第二个do则是动词，译成"做"。"What do you do?"相当于中文的"你／你们是做什么的？"这是特殊疑问句（即疑问词引导的问句）。有关特殊疑问句的造句法请参考第3课。

例 A: What do you do? 你的职业是什么？

B: I'm a teacher. 我是教书的。

A: What does John do? 约翰是从事哪一行的呀？

B: He drives a taxi. 他是开出租车的。

4 Substitution 替换

1. Miss Lin works | for IBM. | 林小姐在 IBM 公司 / 某银行上班。
   | in a bank.

2. What a | coincidence! | 好巧呀 / 真令人惊奇呀!
   | surprise!

3. I'd like you to | meet my friend, Sal. 我想请你见见我的朋友莎儿。
   | call me a <u>cab</u>. 我想请你帮我叫部出租车。 *taxi*
   | give me a <u>call</u>. 我想请你打个电话给我。 *ring/buzz*

4. What | do you do? 你从事哪一行的?
   | is your occupation? 你的职业是什么?
   | is your job? 你的工作是什么?

5. I'm a | secretary. | 我是个秘书 / 老师 / 医生。
   | teacher.
   | doctor.

5 Exercises 练习

I. Use the right word: 请选出适当的单词 :

job	like	works	How
What	do	for	Same

1. How do you __do__, Miss Li?

2. John __works__ in a bank.

3. Tina works __for__ a trading company.

4. I'd __like__ you to meet my friend, Tom.

5. What's your __job__ ?

6. __What__ a nice day!

7. __How__ beautiful she is!

8. __Same__ here.

II. Complete the dialogue: 完成下列会话：

Mr. Li: Miss Wang, t h i s is my friend, Mr. Jones.

Miss Wang: How d o you do, Mr. Jones?

Mr. Jones: How do you do?

Miss Wang: What do you d o , Mr. Jones?

Mr. Jones: I'm a teacher. A n d you?

Miss Wang: I'm a secretary in a trading company.

Mr. Jones: H o w nice! Have a nice day.

Miss Wang: You, t o o .

Lesson 6

Time

时间

会话 A

A: Excuse me, Ma'am. What time is it, please?

B: It's two thirty. *two thirty-one 2:31*

A: Thanks. What time is the next train?

B: Two forty-five.

A: I see. Is it on time?

B: Yes, it is.

A: 小姐，打扰一下。请问现在几点了？

B: 现在是两点半。

A: 谢谢。请问下一班火车是几点开？

B: 2 点 45 分。

A: 我明白了。它准时吗?

B: 是的,它很准时。

会话 B

A: Hi, Tom. What time is it, please?

B: It's a quarter to seven. 6:45. (57:00差 15min)

A: Oh, no! I'm late.

B: It's OK. / It doesn't matter

A: What do you mean?

B: My watch is fast.

A: 嗨,汤姆。请问现在几点了?

B: 现在是 6 点 45 分。

A: 噢,糟了! 我迟到了。

B: 没关系。

A: 你说这话什么意思?

B: 我的表快了。

2 *Vocabulary & Idioms* 单词短语注解

会话 A

1. **Ma'am** [mæm] 名 夫人；小姐（对女性的口头尊称）

2. **time** [taɪm] 名 时间

3. **two** [tu] 名 2

4. **thirty** [ˈθɝtɪ] 名 30

5. **next** [nɛkst] 形 下一个的，其次的

6. **train** [tren] 名 火车

7. **forty-five** [ˌfɔrtɪˈfaɪv] 名 45

8. **I see.** 我明白了。

9. **on time** 准时

会话 B

1. **quarter** [ˈkwɔrtɚ] 名 四分之一；一刻钟（15 分钟）

2. **seven** [ˈsɛvən] 名 7

3. **late** [let] 形 迟的，晚的

4. **mean** [min] 动 意味，表示……的意思

5. **watch** [wɑtʃ] 名 （手）表

6. **fast** [fæst] 形 快的，（钟表）走得快的

3 *Grammar Points* 语法重点

会话 A

1. **What time is it, please?** 请问现在几点了？

   what time do you have?

   = What time is it by your watch, please? 请问你的表现在几点了？
   问句中的 it 是代词，此处代替时间，可表示现在、过去或未来的时间，在本问句中，it 指现在的时间，译成"现在"，不要译成"它"。

请参看下列：

例 A: What time is it, please? 请问现在几点了?
　　B: It's ten in the morning. 现在是早上 10 点。

2. 注意下列表数字的念法：

1	one [wʌn]	2	two [tu]
3	three [θri]	4	four [fɔr]
5	five [faɪv]	6	six [sɪks] Sex
7	seven [ˈsɛvən]	8	eight [et]
9	nine [naɪn]	10	ten [tɛn]
11	eleven [ɪˈlɛvən]	12	twelve [twɛlv]
13	thirteen [θɝˈtin]	14	fourteen [fɔrˈtin]
15	fifteen [fɪfˈtin]	16	sixteen [sɪksˈtin]
17	seventeen [ˌsɛvənˈtin]	18	eighteen [eˈtin]
19	nineteen [naɪnˈtin]	20	twenty [ˈtwɛntɪ]
21	twenty-one [ˌtwɛntɪˈwʌn]	30	thirty [ˈθɝtɪ]
40	forty [ˈfɔrtɪ]	50	fifty [ˈfɪftɪ]
60	sixty [ˈsɪkstɪ]	70	seventy [ˈsɛvəntɪ] thirsty
80	eighty [ˈetɪ]	90	ninety [ˈnaɪntɪ]
100		one hundred [ˈhʌndrəd]	
1,000		one thousand [ˈθauzənd] 10^2	
10,000		ten thousand 10^3	
100,000		one hundred thousand 10^5	
1,000,000		one million [ˈmɪljən] 10^6	

3. 下列亦为表示时间的说法：

a.

It's noon. 现在是中午 12 点。

= It's twelve noon.

或：It's midnight. 现在是午夜 12 点。

= It's twelve midnight.

b.

It's five past three. 现在是 3 点 5 分。

= It's three o five.

注意

（1）此处 o 虽等于中文的"零"，但要念成英文字母"o"的音。

1-9 →（2）"3 点 01 分"至"3 点 09 分"要念成：

"three o one"、"three o two" ... "three o nine"。

→ "10 分"之后均不需加"o"，即：

3 点 10 分 : three ten

3 点 11 分 : three eleven

其他表"几点几分"均以此类推。如：

1 点 02 分 : one o two / two past one

9 点 29 分 : nine twenty-nine / twenty-nine past nine

c. 分针指到"3"时，可念成"fifteen"（15）或"a quarter"。a quarter 原指"四分之一"，60 分的四分之一即 15 分之意。如：

It's one fifteen. 现在是 1 点 15 分。

= It's fifteen past one.

= It's a quarter past one.

但不可说：

✕It's one a quarter.（ × ）

d. 分针指到"6"时，可念成"thirty"（30）或"half"（一半）。如：

It's two thirty. 现在是 2 点 30 分 / 两点半。

= It's half past two.

但不可说：

✕It's two half.（ × ）

e. 分针所指的数字超过"6"，则有下列念法：

It's twenty to five. 现在是差 20 分到 5 点。

= It's four forty. 现在是 4 点 40 分。

It's five to ten. 现在是差 5 分到 10 点

= It's nine fifty-five. 现在是 9 点 55 分。√

f. 准点(即分针指到"12")时,表"几点钟"有下列说法:

It's one o'clock. 现在是 1 点。

= It's one.

It's seven o'clock. 现在是 7 点。

= It's seven.

注意

表示"现在是中午12点/午夜12点"就不必使用"o'clock"一词。

即:

It's twelve noon. (√)

It's twelve midnight. (√)

It's twelve o'clock noon. (o'clock 是赘词)

It's twelve o'clock midnight. (o'clock 是赘词)

4. 精确表示时间时,应念出"时"、"分"、"秒",即:

时:o'clock [ə'klɑk]

分:minute ['mɪnɪt]

秒 : second [ˈsɛkənd]

故若表示"现在是 5 点 20 分 18 秒"理应说成:

It's five o'clock, twenty minutes, and eighteen seconds.

不过这个念法实在是太啰嗦了,故实际应念成:

It's five twenty and eighteen seconds.

5. 表"现在是上午 / 下午 5 点 20 分"应念成:

It's five twenty a.m. 现在是上午 5 点 20 分。

= It's five twenty A.M.

It's five twenty p.m. 现在是下午 5 点 20 分。

= It's five twenty P.M.

注意

a.m. 或 A.M. [ˌeˈɛm] 是拉丁文 ante meridiem(= before midday,午前)的缩写。而 p.m. 或 P.M. [ˌpiˈɛm] 是拉丁文 post meridiem(= after midday,午后)的缩写。现在亦有人省略缩写符号".",直接写成 am / AM 或 pm / PM。

6. **I see.** 我明白了。

= I understand.

see 是动词,原指"看见",如:

I see a cat there. 我看见一只猫在那里。

但 see 亦可表示"明白"、"了解"之意。

例 A: Why can't he come? 他为什么不能来?

B: He is busy. 他很忙。

A: I see. 我明白了。

7. **Is it on time?** 它(这班火车)准时吗?

on time 准时

例 The train is never late. It is always on time.

这班火车从未晚点,它向来都很准时。

会话 B

1. **What do you mean?** 你这是什么意思?

mean 是动词,相当中文"意味"、"指的是"之意。

例 A: John is a lazybones. 约翰是个懒骨头。

B: What do you mean? 你这话什么意思？

A: He is a lazy guy. 他是个懒家伙。

* lazybones [ˈlezɪˌbonz] 名 懒骨头，懒人（lazybones 是单复数同形的名词，即：a lazybones、two lazybones）

* lazy [ˈlezɪ] 形 懒惰的；guy [gaɪ] 名 家伙（男性）

2. **My watch is fast.** 我的表快了。

My watch is slow. 我的表慢了。

在上列句型中，fast 或 slow 之前可置表示时间的名词，分别表示"快 / 慢若干时间"。

例 My watch is ten minutes fast. 我的表快了 10 分钟。

The alarm clock is two hours slow. 这个闹钟慢了两个小时。

4 **Substitution** 替换 ♋

1. | What time is it, please? 请问现在几点了？
| What time is it by your watch, please? 请问你的表现在几点了？

2. It's | two thirty.　　　现在是 2 点 30 分。
| two (o'clock).　现在是 2 点钟。
| ten a.m.　　　现在是上午 10 点。
| one p.m.　　　现在是下午 1 点。

3. It's | a quarter to seven. 现在是 7 点差 15 分。
| six forty-five.　　现在是 6 点 45 分。

4. It's | twenty past five. 现在是 5 点 20 分。
| five twenty.

5. My watch is | fast.　　　　　　我的表快了。
| one hour fast.　　我的表快了 1 个小时。
| slow.　　　　　　我的表慢了。
| ten minutes slow. 我的表慢了 10 分钟。

5

Exercises 练习

I. Use the right word: 请选出适当的单词：

o	quarter	it	time
midnight	watch	next	half

1. What time is _it_, please?
2. It's _half_ past three.
3. What time is the _next_ bus?
4. Is it on _time_ ?
5. It's a _quarter_ to two.
6. My _watch_ is fast.
7. It's six _o_ five.
8. It's twelve _midnight_

II. Complete the dialogue: 完成下列会话：

A: What time is it b _y_ your watch?

B: It's twelve n_oon_ .

A: Oh, no! I'm l _ate_ .

B: Why?

A: My bus is always on t _ime_ .

B: I s _ee_ . Don't worry.

A: What do you m _ean_ ?

B: My watch is twenty minutes f _ast_ .

A: Thank God! So it's twenty t _o_ twelve.

Lesson 7

Day and Date
日期

Dialogue 会话

会话 A

A: What <u>day</u> is it today, Tom? *time*

B: It's Sunday.

A: And is today June 6? *6th.*

B: Yes. Why?

A: Because it's my birthday.

B: Happy birthday, May.

A: Thanks.

A: 汤姆，今天是星期几?

B: 今天是星期日。

A: 那么今天是不是 6 月 6 日?

B: 是啊。为什么这样问呢？

A: 因为今天是我的生日。

B: 生日快乐，梅。

A: 谢了。

会话 B

A: <u>What's today's date</u>, Tom?

B: It's February 14.

A: What day is it today?

B: It's Friday.

A: No, it's not. It's Valentine's Day.

B: Happy Valentine's Day, May.

A: 汤姆，今天是几月几号？

B: 今天是 2 月 14 号。

A: 那今天是什么日子呢？

B: 今天是星期五。

A: 不，才不是呢。今天是情人节。

B: 情人节快乐，梅。

2 *Vocabulary & Idioms* 单词短语注解

会话 A

1. **day** [de] 名 日子

2. **today** [təˈde] 名 今天

3. **Sunday** [ˈsʌndɪ] 名 星期日

4. **June** [dʒun] 名 6 月

5. **because** [bɪˈkɔz] 连 因为
   Because he is nice, I like him. 因为他人很好,所以我喜欢他。

6. **my** [maɪ] 代 我的

7. **birthday** [ˈbɜθˌde] 名 生日

8. **happy** [ˈhæpɪ] 形 快乐的;Happy birthday. 生日快乐。

会话 B

1. **date** [det] 名 日期

2. **February** [ˈfɛbruˌɛrɪ] 名 2 月

3. **Friday** [ˈfraɪdɪ] 名 星期五

4. **Valentine's Day** 圣瓦伦丁节(2 月 14 日情人节)
   Valentine [ˈvæləntaɪn] 名 圣·瓦伦丁(公元 3 世纪时罗马基督教殉教者)

3 *Grammar Points* 语法重点

会话 A

1. **What day is it today, Tom?** 汤姆,今天是星期几?

   a. 这是个很实用的句型,此处的 it 是代词,作主语,与 "What time is it?" 中的 it 完全相同,是表示时间的词,若采用逐字翻译,本问句实应译成:

今天（today）现在（it）是（is）什么日子（what day）？

不过实际上 it 是不必译出的。同样地，我们也可使用这个句型产生下列的问句：

What day is it <u>tomorrow</u>? 明天星期几？

What day is it <u>the day after tomorrow</u>? 后天星期几？

b. 在 "What day is it today?" 的问句中，我们亦可将 it 省略，直接用 today 作主语，即：

What day is it today?

= What day is <u>today</u>?

同理：

What day is it tomorrow?

= What day is <u>tomorrow</u>?

What day is it the day after tomorrow?

= What day is <u>the day after tomorrow</u>?

c. 由于问句有上列变化，因此答句亦有下列变化：

A: What day is it today? 今天是星期几？

B: It's Monday（today）. 今天星期一。

或：

A: What day is <u>today</u>?

B: <u>Today</u> is Monday.

d. 下列为"星期一"至"星期日"的念法：

Monday [ˈmʌndɪ] 星期一　　Tuesday [ˈtjuzdɪ] 星期二

Wednesday [ˈwɛnzdɪ] 星期三　Thursday [ˈθɝzdɪ] 星期四

Friday [ˈfraɪdɪ] 星期五　　Saturday [ˈsætədɪ] 星期六

Sunday [ˈsʌndɪ] 星期日

注意

中国人习惯将星期一视为一个星期中的第一天，星期日则为最后一天。但西方人则是将星期日作为第一天，星期六则为最后一天。即：

Sunday → Monday → Tuesday → Wednesday → Thursday → Friday → Saturday

例 A: What's the first day of the week?

一星期的第一天是哪一天？

B: It's Sunday. 是星期天。

2. **And is today June 6?** 那么今天是不是 6 月 6 日？

a. 下列为英文月份的念法：

January [ˈdʒænjuˌɛrɪ] 1 月 　　February [ˈfɛbruˌɛrɪ] 2 月

March [mɑrtʃ] 3 月 　　April [ˈeprəl] 4 月

May [me] 5 月 　　June [dʒun] 6 月

July [dʒuˈlaɪ] 7 月 　　August [ˈɔgəst] 8 月

September [sɛpˈtɛmbɚ] 9 月 　　October [ɑkˈtobɚ] 10 月

November [noˈvɛmbɚ] 11 月 　　December [dɪˈsɛmbɚ] 12 月

b. 若表示"1998 年 6 月 6 日"，英文要写成：

June 6, 1998

同理，"1999 年 3 月 2 日"应写成：

March 2, 1999

注意

上列日期中的阿拉伯数字不是基数（即 one，two，three... 一、二、三……），而是序数（即 first，second，third... 第一、第二、第三……）。故"June 6, 1998"要念成：

June sixth, nineteen ninety-eight（口语）

= June the sixth, nineteen ninety-eight（较正式，美式用法）

= the sixth (day) of June, nineteen ninety-eight（正式，英式用法）

以上三种念法中，以第一种最为口语，也最为常用。

3. 序数词就是表示次序（第一、第二、第三……）的数词，请参看下列序数词的写法：

first [fɝst] 第一 　　second [ˈsɛkənd] 第二

third [θɝd] 第三 　　fourth [fɔrθ] 第四

fifth [fɪfθ] 第五 　　sixth [sɪksθ] 第六

seventh [ˈsɛvənθ] 第七 　　eighth [etθ] 第八

ninth [naɪnθ] 第九 　　tenth [tɛnθ] 第十

eleventh [ɪˈlɛvənθ] 第十一 　　twelfth [twɛlfθ] 第十二

thirteenth [θɝˈtinθ] 第十三 　　fourteenth [fɔrˈtinθ] 第十四

fifteenth [fɪfˈtinθ] 第十五 　　sixteenth [sɪksˈtinθ] 第十六

seventeenth [ˌsɛvənˈtinθ] 第十七 　　eighteenth [eˈtinθ] 第十八

nineteenth [ˌnaɪnˈtinθ] 第十九　　twentieth [ˈtwɛntɪθ] 第二十
twenty-first [ˌtwɛntɪˈfɜst] 第二十一　　thirtieth [ˈθɜtɪθ] 第三十
fortieth [ˈfɔrtɪθ] 第四十　　fiftieth [ˈfɪftɪθ] 第五十
sixtieth [ˈsɪkstɪθ] 第六十　　seventieth [ˈsɛvəntɪθ] 第七十
eightieth [ˈetɪθ] 第八十　　ninetieth [ˈnaɪntɪθ] 第九十
one hundredth [ˈhʌndrədθ] 第一百

4.　基数词与序数词的区别：
　　基数词是用来表示数量，序数词则是用来表示次序。
　　例 He has <u>five</u> books. 他有五本书。
　　　I like the <u>fifth</u> book. 我喜欢第五本书。

5.　**Happy birthday, May.** 梅，祝你生日快乐。
　　这是在某人生日时所使用的祝贺语。原句亦可说成：
　　Happy birthday <u>to you</u>, May.

会话 B

1.　**What's today's date, Tom?** 汤姆，今天是几月几号？
　　上列问句中，date 表"日期"，而会话 A 中的 day 则指"星期几"，
　　请比较下列对话：
　　A: What's today's date? 今天是几月几号？
　　B: It's March 3. 今天是 3 月 3 号。
　　A: What day is it today? 今天是星期几？
　　B: It's Saturday. 今天是星期六。
　　注意
　　表示"今天是几月几号？"习惯说成：
　　What's today's date?
　= What's the date today?
　　而不要说成：
　　What date is it today? (×)
　　What date is today? (×)
　　但表示"今天是星期几？"则习惯说成：
　　What day is it today?
　= What day is today?

而不要说成：

What's today's day? (×)

What's the day today? (×)

2. 所有格的形态及用法：

a. What's today's date? 今天是几月几号？

上列问句中，today's 是所有格，译成"今天的"。

所谓"所有格"就是一种有限定作用的形容词，表示"属于……的"之意，之后要置名词。如：

<u>my</u> book 我的书（属于我的书）

<u>John's</u> father 约翰的爸爸（属于约翰的爸爸）

<u>the boy's</u> toy 这个男孩的玩具（属于这个男孩的玩具）

<u>today's</u> date 今天的日期（属于今天的日期）

b. 所有格的形态：

（1）代词所有格（由代词形成）

代词		代词所有格
第一人称	I 我	my 我的
	we 我们	our 我们的
第二人称	you 你	your 你的
	you 你们	your 你们的
第三人称	he 他	his 他的
	she 她	her 她的
	it 它	its 它的
	they 他/她/它们	their 他/她/它们的

例 Where's <u>your</u> school? 你的学校在哪儿？

<u>His</u> father is an English teacher. 他的爸爸是位英文老师。

They must do <u>their</u> work now.

他们现在必须做他们的工作。

（2）人或动物名词所有格（由名词加"s"形成）此类名词均指人或动物，分成专有名词及普通名词两种：

专有名词（即某人所专有的姓名）：

John（约翰）、Mr. Wang（王先生）

普通名词

the man（这名男子）、a woman（某妇女）、a girl（某女孩子）、
his son（他的儿子）、the dog（这只狗）

以上名词加了"s"即形成所有格，如：

John's father   约翰的爸爸
Mr. Wang's wife   王先生的太太
the man's car   这名男子的车
a girl's mother   一位女孩的妈妈
the girls' mother   那些女孩的妈妈
the dog's tail   这只狗的尾巴

注意

（a）若普通名词为复数（字尾有"s"），其所有格形态为：

    This is a girls' school. 这是一所女子学校。

= This is a school for girls.

    不要写成：

    This is a girl's school.

  * 比较下列各句的不同：

    This is a girls' school. 这是一所女子学校。

    This is a girl's school. 这是某个女孩子所上的学校。

    This is the girls' school. 这是那些女孩子所上的学校。

    This is the girl's school. 这是那个女孩子所上的学校。

（b）若专有名词本身就有"s"，形成所有格时有两种变化：

    专有名词：Mr. Jones 琼斯先生

    所有格：Mr. Jones' car 琼斯先生的车子

        = Mr. Jones's car

  * Jones' 或 Jones's 均念成 [ˈdʒonzɪz]

（3）若名词代表的是人或动物以外所有无生命的东西或植物
时，则通常不使用上列所有格形态，而要采用下列结构：

the A of B   B 的 A

the color of the table   桌子的颜色
the roof of the house   房子的屋顶
the leaves of the tree   这棵树的叶子

不可写成：

the table's color

the house's roof

the tree's leaves

（4）不过表示时间或地方的名词却可采用两种所有格形态：

时间名词

today（今天）、tomorrow（明天）、yesterday（昨天）

所有格

today's world 今天的世界

= the world (of) today

yesterday's weather 昨天的天气

= the weathe (of) yesterday

地方名词

city（城市）、country（国家）、Hong Kong（香港）、Canada（加拿大）

所有格

the city's traffic 该城市的交通

= the traffic of the city

Canada's climate 加拿大的气候

= the climate of Canada

c.　以上有关所有格的要点均为基本提示，看似繁琐，实则并不是那么困难，务请读者配合本书认真学习，假以时日一定可以练就踏实的语法基础。

4　　　　**Substitution 替换**　　　　♋

1.　What day is it │today?
　　　　　　　　　│tomorrow?　　今天／明天是星期几？

 =　What day is │today?
　　　　　　　　│tomorrow?

2.　It's Sunday │today.
　　　　　　　　│tomorrow.　　今天／明天是星期日。

 =　Today
　　Tomorrow │is Sunday.

3. Is today |June 6? / July 7? 今天是不是 6 月 6 日 /7 月 7 日？

4. Happy |birthday. / New Year. 生日快乐 / 新年快乐。

5. What's |today's date? / the date today? 今天是几月几号？

6. It's |February 14, 1999.
February fourteenth, nineteen ninety-nine.
February the fourteenth, nineteen ninety-nine.
the fourteenth of February, nineteen ninety-nine.

今天是 1999 年 2 月 14 日。

5 Exercises 练习

I. Use the right word: 请选出适当的单词：

our	girls'	day	it
your	today	today's	sixth

1. What _day_ is today?
2. What's _today's_ date?
3. This is a _girls'_ school, not a boys' school.
4. What day is _it_ tomorrow?
5. The weather _today_ is terrible.
6. You must do _your_ homework now.
7. Today is June _sixth_, 1998.
8. We have a nice car. It is _our_ car.

II. Complete the dialogue: 完成下列会话：

A: What's today's d_ate_ ?

B: I_t's_ November 13, 1998. W_hy_ do you ask?

A: B_ecause_ it's Friday.

B: So?

A: Friday t_he_ thirteenth is bad luck.

B: Oh! I see.

Lesson 8

The Weather
天气

会话 *What's the weather like today?*

be+doing 在进行时

A: Hi, May! I am calling from New York.

B: New York! What are you doing there?

A: I'm here on business.

B: How's the weather in New York?

A: It's terrible. It's raining right now.

B: What a shame! *shame on you.*

pity!

62

A: 嗨，梅！我是从纽约打电话来的。

B: 纽约！你在那里做什么啊？

A: 我是来出差的。

B: 纽约的天气怎么样？

A: 糟透了。现在正在下雨呢。

B: 真可惜！

阅读

There are four seasons in my hometown. It's cool in spring. It's sunny in summer. It's chilly in fall. In winter, it is very cold. Sometimes it even snows.

我家乡有四个季节。春天的天气凉爽，夏天阳光普照，秋天寒冷，而冬天则是非常冷，有时甚至还会下雪呢。

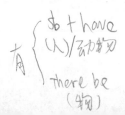

② *Vocabulary & Idioms* 单词短语注解 ✎

会话

1. **call** [kɔl] 动打电话（calling 是 call 的现在分词）

2. **New York** [ˌnjuˋjɔrk] 名纽约（地名，位于美国东部）

3. **on business** 出差
   business [ˋbɪznɪs] 名商业，事业，生意
   My father will go to Hong Kong on business tomorrow.
   我爸爸明天要去香港出差。

4. **weather** [ˋwɛðɚ] 名天气

5. **terrible** [ˋtɛrəbḷ] 形很糟糕的；恐怖的   *awful*

6. **rain** [ren] 动下雨（raining 是 rain 的现在分词）

7. **right now** 现在
   right [raɪt] 副立刻，马上（强调用法）
   now [naʊ] 副现在（时间副词）

8. **What a shame!** 真可惜 / 遗憾！
   = What a pity!
   shame [ʃem] 名可惜的事，憾事
   pity [ˋpɪtɪ] 名可惜的事，憾事
   A: I can't go with you to the picnic. 我不能和你们去野餐。
   B: What a shame! 真可惜！

阅读

1. **there are** + 复数名词　有……

2. **season** [ˋsizn̩] 名季节

3. **hometown** [ˌhomˋtaʊn] 名家乡，故乡

4. **cool** [kul] 形凉（爽）的

5. **spring** [sprɪŋ] 名 春天

6. **sunny** [ˈsʌnɪ] 形 出太阳的，有阳光的

7. **summer** [ˈsʌmɚ] 名 夏天

8. **chilly** [ˈtʃɪlɪ] 形 寒冷的

9. **fall** [fɔl] 名 秋天 (美式用法)
   = autumn [ˈɔtəm] (英式用法)

10. **winter** [ˈwɪntɚ] 名 冬天

11. **very** [ˈvɛrɪ] 副 非常地，很

12. **cold** [kold] 形 (寒) 冷的

13. **sometimes** [ˈsʌmˌtaɪmz] 副 有时候

14. **even** [ˈivən] 副 甚至

15. **snow** [sno] 动 下雪

3 *Grammar Points* 语法重点 〜〜〜

会话

本会话旨在介绍现在进行时的形态及用法。

1. 现在进行时的形态：

   I am calling from New York. 我正从纽约打电话过来。

   What are you doing there? 你正在那里做什么？

   It's (= It is) raining right now. 现在正在下雨。

   以上各句均属现在进行时的结构。

2. 何谓现在进行时？

   现在进行时就是一种用来表示"在现在的时刻，某动作正在进行"的状态，相当于中文的"（现在）正在……"之意。其结构如下：

   主语＋现在时的 be 动词＋现在分词　……正在……

   * 现在时的 be 动词即：is、am、are。

   * 现在分词由"动词＋ing"形成，即：

动词			现在分词
call	打电话	→	calling
do	(做)事	→	doing
rain	下雨	→	raining
sing	唱歌	→	singing
dance	跳舞	→	dancing

3. 何时使用现在进行时？

   只要想表达相当于中文"现在正在……"的概念时，就可使用现在进行时。

   例 Mary is singing in the room. 玛丽正在房间里唱歌。

   Tom is dancing with Mary. 汤姆正在与玛丽跳舞。

   I'm (= I am) writing a letter. 我正在写一封信。

   They're (= They are) doing the work. 他们正在做那件工作。

   换言之，只要中文可说"正在……"时，英文就可使用进行时，否则便不能使用进行时。这里以动词 have (有) 为例：

   有此中文说法：我有钱。(√)

   故亦有此英文说法：I have money. (√)

   无此中文说法：我正在有钱。(×)

   故亦无此英文说法：I'm having money. (×)   中英相通

   have 除表"有"之外，亦可表"吃(饭)"之意。

   有此中文说法：我正在吃晚餐。(√)

   故亦有此英文说法：I'm having dinner. (√)

   由上得知，就"现在进行时"而言，中英文是相通的。只要本着上述原则，我们就可精确掌握现在进行时使用的时机。

4. **It's raining right now.**

   = It's raining now.

   现在正在下雨。

   上列句子中，right now 及 now 意思相同，均译成"现在"，只不过 now 之前置 right 有强调的功能，相当于"就在现在"。

   例 A: Where's Peter? 彼得在哪里？

   B: He is studying in the library (right) now.

他现在正在图书馆看书。

不过由于现在进行时本身即已表示"现在"的时刻，故句尾的 now
或 right now 亦可省略。故：

He is studying in the library（ right ）now.

= He is studying in the library.

It's raining right now.

= It's raining.

5. **How's the weather in New York?** 纽约的天气怎么样?

表示"某地的天气如何?"有下列两种说法：

How's (= How is) the weather in + 地方?

= What's (= What is) the weather like in + 地方?

例 How's the weather in Tokyo today? 东京今天的天气如何?

= What's the weather like in Tokyo today?

阅读

本短文旨在介绍"有"及若干修饰天气的常用形容词。

1. **There are four seasons in my hometown.**

我的家乡有四个季节。

上句中，there are 译成"有"。

中文里，主语不论是人或地方、事物，均使用相同的动词"有"。

例 我 有一本书。

　　人

　　这只猴子 有条长尾巴。

　　　　动物

　　我的家乡 有四个季节。

　　　地方

　　桌上有一本书。

　　物

　　一年 有 12 个月。

　　时间

但在英文中，表"有"时，除了动词 have 以外，尚有 there is / there

are, 这些不同用法经常造成初学英文者的困扰。其实分辨"有"的用法并不难, 其详述如下:

a. 中文句首为"人"或"动物", 应使用 have。

例 我有一本书。("我"是人)

→ I have a book. (√)

这只猴子有条长尾巴。("猴子"是动物)

→ The monkey has a long tail.

b. 中文句首是"场所"(如: 车上、屋内、树林里)或"时间"时, 就须使用 there is / there are。句型如下:

$$
\left|\begin{array}{l}\text{there is + 单数名词}\\ \text{there are + 复数名词}\end{array}\right| + \left|\begin{array}{l}\text{in(在……之内)}\\ \text{on(在……之上)}\\ \text{by(在……旁边)}\\ \text{near(在……附近)}\end{array}\right| + \text{名词}
$$

例 桌上有本书。

On the desk has a book. (×)

→ There is a book on the desk. (√)

1 年有 12 个月。

In a year has twelve months. (×)

→ There are twelve months in a year. (√)

同理:

树上有只鸟。

→ There is a bird on the tree. (√)

我家附近有一所学校。

→ There is a school near my house. (√)

试译下列各句:

(1)一星期有 7 天。

(2)窗(window)边有个花瓶(vase)。

(3)袋子(bag)里有一些书。

(4)车站(station)旁边有棵大树。

参考译句:

(1)There are seven days in a week.

(2)There is a vase by the window.

（3）There are some books in the bag.

（4）There is a big tree by the station.

2. 在以 **"there is / there are"** 起首的句型中，应将 **there is** 或 **there are** 视为固定的用语，译成"有"，而不要译成"那里是"。若要表示"那里/这里有……"时，应采用下列句型：

there is + 单数名词 + there / here

there are + 复数名词 + there / here

译 那里有个人。

不可说：

There is a man.（本句只表示"有个人"。）

更不可说：

There has a man.（无此用法）

而要说：

There is a man there.（√）

译 这里有五个苹果。

There are five apples here.（√）

3. 修饰天气的形容词常用的如下：

sunny ['sʌnɪ]	出太阳的，有阳光的
rainy ['renɪ]	下雨的
cloudy ['klaʊdɪ]	有云的，阴天的
windy ['wɪndɪ]	有风的，风大的
snowy ['snoɪ]	有雪的，下雪的
foggy ['fɑgɪ]	起雾的，雾大的
chilly ['tʃɪlɪ]	寒冷的，冷飕飕的
cold [kold]	寒冷的（比 chilly 更冷）
cool [kul]	凉的，凉爽的
hot [hɑt]	炎热的
warm [wɔrm]	温暖的

例 A: What's the weather like today? 今天天气怎么样？

B: It's cold and rainy. 又冷又下雨。

4. 代词 **it** 可用以表示"天气"。

在稍早的会话中，我们曾介绍代词 it 可用以代替任何单数的名词、时间。在本课中，我们亦发现 it 可用以表示天气，相当于"the weather"之意。

a. 代替单数的名词：

例 I have a dog. It (= The dog) is big and strong.

我有一条狗，它长得又大又壮。

b. 代替时间：

例 It's Monday today. 今天是星期一。

= Today is Monday.

c. 代替天气：

例 It's cool today. 今天的天气凉爽。

= The weather is cool today.

5. 比较下列两句的不同：

It's rainy today. 今天天气是雨天。

It's raining now. 现在正在下雨。

上列第一句中，rainy 是形容词，表示"下雨的"，强调下雨的"现象"。raining 则是现在分词，与之前的 is 形成现在进行时"is raining"，表示"正在下雨"，强调下雨的"动作"。

4 Substitution 替换

1. | I am calling from New York. 我正从纽约打电话过来。
   | Helen is watching TV now. 海伦现在正在看电视。
   | My mother is cooking dinner. 我妈妈正在做晚饭。

2. How's the weather | in New York? 纽约的天气怎么样？
   What's the weather like |

3. There are four seasons in my hometown. 我家乡有四个季节。
   There is a painting on the wall. 墙上有一幅画。
   There are many stores near my house. 我家附近有许多商店。

4. There is a dictionary | there. | 那里 / 这里有一本词典。
                          | here. |

5. It's | cool
        | cold | today. 今天天气凉爽 / 寒冷 / 炎热。
        | hot

6. It's a | sunny
         | rainy | day. 今天是晴天 / 雨天 / 阴天。
         | cloudy

5 Exercises 练习

I. Use the right word: 请选出适当的单词 :

have ✓	has ✓	having ✓	doing
is ✓	It's ✓	are ✓	like ✓

1. I'm _having_ dinner right now.
2. What's the weather _like_ in Beijing?
3. There _are_ two books on the desk.
4. The dog _has_ a big mouth.
5. _It's_ rainy today.
6. I _have_ no money.
7. There _is_ a big tree near my house.
8. What are you _doing_ here?

II. Complete the dialogue: 完成下列会话：

A: What a h o t day!

B: Well, it is s ummer now.

A: Does it r ain in summer?

B: Yes. Why?

A: I like r ainy days.

B: That's strange. Why?

A: It'll be c ool .

B: I s ee .

A: Hey! Look! It's r aining.

Lesson 9

可以多人

Telephone Conversation I

电话会话(一)

1 *Dialogue* 会话

只限两人

会话A

A: Hello! May I speak to Bob, please?

B: He's not in.

A: May I leave a message?

B: Sure. Go ahead.

A: This is Tom. Please ask him to call me back as soon as possible.

B: OK. Bye.

A: 你好！请问我可以跟鲍勃说话吗？

B: 他不在。

A: 我可以留个话吗？

B: 当然。请说吧。

A: 我是汤姆。请他尽快给我回电话。

B: 好的。再见。

会话 B

A: May I speak to Mr. Wang, please?

B: Who's calling, please?

A: This is Tom Lin.

B: Hold on, please. (a few seconds later) He's out at the moment.

A: When will he be back?

B: I don't know.

A: OK. I'll call back later. Bye.

A: 请问我可以跟王先生说话吗?

B: 请问是谁呀?

A: 我是林汤姆。

B: 请稍等一下。（几秒钟后）他现在出去了。

A: 他什么时候会回来呢?

B: 我不知道。

A: 好吧。我稍后再打来。再见。

② *Vocabulary & Idioms* 单词短语注解 ✎

会话 A

1. **telephone** [ˈtɛləˌfon] 名 电话（机）

2. **conversation** [ˌkɑnvəˈseʃən] 名 会话，谈话

3. **hello** [həˈlo] 叹 哈啰（招呼语）

4. **speak to** + 人　跟某人说话
   speak [spik] 动 说话，讲

5. **Bob** [bɑb] 名 鲍勃（男子名）

6. **in** [ɪn] 副 在家；在办公室

7. **leave a message** 留话
   leave [liv] 动 留下
   message [ˈmɛsɪdʒ] 名 传言；信息

8. **sure** [ʃʊr] 副 当然

9. **go ahead** （电话）请说话
   ahead [əˈhɛd] 副 在前（面），在先

10. **ask** + 人 + **to** + 动词　请某人（做……）
    ask [æsk] 动 请求

11. **back** [bæk] 副 回原处；回来

12. **as soon as possible** 尽快（地）
    as [æz] 副 一样地 & 连 和
    soon [sun] 副 快
    possible [ˈpɑsəbḷ] 形 可能的

会话 B

1. **Wang** [wɑŋ] 名 王（姓氏）

2. **hold on** （打电话时）等着，别挂断
   hold [hold] 动 保持（某种姿势）；拿，握

3. **a few** + 名词 一些……

   注意

   few [fju] 形 与不定冠词 a 连用形成 a few 时,为肯定用法,表"一些";若前面不加 a 时,则为否定用法,表"很少的"、"不多的"。

   He has a few friends. 他有一些朋友。

   He has few friends. 他没什么朋友。

4. **out** [aʊt] 副 外出

5. **at the moment** 此刻,现在

   moment ['momənt] 名 瞬间;某一时刻

6. **know** [no] 动 知道

7. **call back** 再回电话,再打电话来

③ *Grammar Points* 语法重点 〜〜

会话 A

本课旨在介绍助动词(如 may、will 等)的用法。

1. 何谓助动词?

   顾名思义,助动词就是一种帮助动词的词类,置于动词之前,以加强动词的语气。

   要了解英文的助动词,就要先了解中文的助动词。

   中文:

   我明天会见你。

   他能做这事。

   你现在可以走了。

   在上列句中,"会"、"能"、"可以"是助动词,分别置于动词"见"、"做"、"走"之前。

   以上各句若译成英文,则为:

   I will see you tomorrow.

   He can do it.

   You may go now.

will、can 及 may 均为助动词，分别置于动词 see、do、go 之前。

2. 助动词在句中的位置

由上得知，中英文均会使用到助动词，且在上述陈述句中，不论中文或英文，助动词均置于动词之前。唯在问句中，助动词所放的位置则有明显的差异。

中文：你明天<u>会</u>见我吗？

你<u>能</u>做这事吗？

我现在<u>可以</u>走了吗？

英文：<u>Will</u> you <u>see</u> me tomorrow?

<u>Can</u> you <u>do</u> it?

<u>May</u> I <u>go</u> now?

由上得知，在中文中，不论陈述句或问句，助动词均置于动词之前；但在英文问句中，助动词则须置于句首，之后接主语，再接动词原形。

3. 以下是英文中常用的助动词：

may（可以）, can（能够、可以）, will（将要、将会）, must（必须）, should（应该 / 当）, shall（要）。

这里将这些助动词的用法介绍如下：

a. may　可以

(1) 若使用于问句中，may 多与主语 I 连用，句型如下：

May I＋动词原形？　我可以……吗？（语气客气）

May I＋动词原形, please?

请问我可以……吗？（语气更客气）

说话者想做某件事，礼貌上欲征求对方同意时，即可使用本句型。

例　May I open the window? 我可以打开窗户吗？

May I sit here, please? 请问我可以坐在这里吗？

本课会话中的"May I speak to Bob, please?"（请问我可以跟鲍勃说话吗？）及"May I leave a message?"（我可以留个话吗？）均属此用法。

(2) 若使用于陈述句中时，may 仍译成"可以"，主语则不限于

I, 句型如下：

主语 (He, You, Mary...) + may + 动词原形

……可以……

长辈或地位高者准许晚辈或地位低者行使某件事时,即可使用本句型。

例 You may leave now. 你现在可以离开了。

He may stay here. 他可以留在这里。

b. can　能够,可以

(1) 表"能够、会"时, can 用以强调一个人的能力。句型如下：

主语 + can + 动词原形　……能够……

Can + 主语 + 动词原形?　……能够……吗?

例 I can do it. 我会做这事。

Can she sing? 她会唱歌吗?

(2) 表"可以"时, can 与 may 的意思及用法均相同。

例 May I open the window? 我可以打开窗户吗?

= Can I open the window?

You may go now. 你可以走了。

= You can go now.

故本课会话中的：

May I speak to Bob, please?

= Can I speak to Bob, please?

May I leave a message?

= Can I leave a message?

c. will　将要,将会

本助动词用以表示未来将发生的事情。句型如下：

主语 + will + 动词原形　……即将……

Will + 主语 + 动词原形?　……即将……吗?

例 He will come today. 他今天会来。

Will it rain tomorrow? 明天会下雨吗?

d. must　必须

本助动词用以表示应当履行的义务,通常只用在陈述句中。

例 You must do it. 你必须做这事。

Everyone must leave now. 每个人现在都必须离开。

e. should　应该/当

本助动词亦用以表示应当履行的义务,语气比 must 弱一些。

例 You should do it. 你应当做这事。

We should study English. 我们应当学英文。

f. shall　要

本助动词通常与主语 I 连用,使用于下列问句:

Shall I...?　要不要我……?

这个句型主要是用来主动表示为对方做某件事。

例 Shall I open the window? 要不要我把窗户打开呀?

Shall I close the door for you? 要不要我替你把门关起来呀?

4. **He's not in.** 他不在。

本句亦可等于 "He is not here."。

5. 下列为表"留话"的电话用语:

May I leave a message? 我可以留话吗?

May I take a message? 我可以帮你留话吗?

例 A: May I leave a message?

B: Sure. Go ahead.

A: Please tell John to meet me at five.

A: 我可以留话吗?

B: 当然。请说吧。

A: 请告诉约翰 5 点跟我见面。

A: Is John there, please?

B: Sorry. He is not in. May I take a message?

A: Don't bother. I'll call back later.

A: 请问约翰在那里吗?

B: 抱歉。他不在。我可以帮你留话吗?

A: 不必麻烦了。我待会再打来。

* bother [ˈbɑðɚ] 动 麻烦

6. **This is Tom.** 我是汤姆。

a. 两人面对面相见时,表示"我是……"一定要说"I am..."。

79

例 A: Who are you? I don't know you. 你是谁？我不认识你。

　　B: I'm John. 我是约翰。

b.　两人若没面对面相见，表"我是……"时则不能说"I am ..."，而
　　要说"This is..."或"It's..."。这种情形用于以下两种情况：

（1）打电话时：

例 A: Who's this, please?（非"Who are you, please?"）

　　= Who's calling, please? 请问是谁呀？

　　B: This is John.（非"I'm John."）我是约翰。

　　= It's John.

（2）在屋内听到门外有人敲门时：

例 A: Who's it, please?（非"Who are you, please?"）

　　B: It's John.（非"I'm John."）

　　A: 请问是谁呀？

　　B: 我是约翰。

7. **This is he.** 我就是。

本句亦是电话用语，常使用于下列对话中：

例 A: Hello. Is John there, please?

　　B: This is he.（非"I am."）Who's calling, please?

　　A: 你好。请问约翰在那儿吗？

　　B: 我就是。请问你是谁呀？

8. **as soon as possible** 尽快（地）　ASAP

这是一个固定的短语。第一个 as 是副词，译成"一样地"，soon
是副词，译成"快"，第二个 as 是副词连接词，译成"和"，possible
则是形容词，译成"可能的"。翻译时，先译 as possible，再译 as
soon，即成"和可能一样地快"，实际则译成"尽快（地）"。这个短语
使用时多置于句尾。

例 You must come back as soon as possible. 你必须尽快回来。

　　Call me as soon as possible. 尽快打电话给我。

会话 B

1. 在电话上，表"请稍候"有下列用语：

Hold on, please.

Just a minute, please.

Just a moment, please.

Wait a minute, please.

Wait a moment, please.

以上用语中，除 "Hold on, please." 仅可使用在电话用语中外，其余四个则不受此限制。

例 A: Hello, this is John. Can I speak to Peter?

B: Hold on, please./Just a minute, please.

A: 你好，我是约翰。我可以跟彼得说话吗?

B: 请稍候。

A: Can I come in? 我可以进来吗?

B: Just a minute, please. (非 "Hold on, please.") 请稍候。

2. **He is out <u>at the moment</u>.** 他此刻不在 / 外出了。

= He is out (<u>now</u>).

---

4   *Substitution* 替换   🦀

1. May / Can | I speak to Bob, please? 请问我可以跟鲍勃说话吗?

2. May I | leave a message? 我可以留个话吗?
sit down? 我可以坐下吗?
ask you a question? 我可以问你一个问题吗?

3. This is / It's | Tom. 我是汤姆。

4. Please ask him to call me back | as soon as possible.
You must see the doctor
I will finish my homework

请他尽快回电话给我。

你必须尽快去看医生。

我会尽快做完家庭作业。

5. Hold on, please.

= Just | a | minute, | please. 请稍候。
Wait | | moment, |

5 **Exercises** 练习 ☾★

I. Use the right word: 请选出适当的单词:

take	Will	This	a
out	May	Few	as

1. _will_ you come tomorrow?

2. _May_ I leave a message?

3. Hello. _This_ is Bill. Who's speaking, please?

4. Can you _take_ a message, please?

5. Sorry. She's _out_ at the moment.

6. _Few_ people know me.

7. I have _a_ few books in my bag.

8. Please come _as_ soon as possible.

II. Complete the dialogue: 完成下列会话:

A: Hello! Is Dan t_here_, please?

B: I'm sorry. He's out at the m_oment_.

A: May I leave a m_essage_?

B: Sure. Who's c_alling_, please?

A: T_his_ is May.

B: H_old_ on, please. OK. Go a_head_.

A: Can you a_sk_ him to call me back?

B: No problem.

Lesson 10

Telephone Conversation II

电话会话(二)

1   *Dialogue* 会话

会话 A

A: Hello, Dr. Chen's <u>clinic</u>. May I help you?

B: Yes, please. I'd like to make an appointment to see Dr. Chen.

                date (personal)

A: What's your name, please?

B: My name is Micky Chen.

A: Is 4 o'clock in the afternoon OK? / alright

B: That's fine. Thank you.

A: 你好，这里是陈医生诊所。我可以帮您什么忙吗？

B: 是的，麻烦你。我想约见陈医生。

A: 请问尊姓大名？

B: 我的名字是陈米奇。

A: 下午 4 点钟可以吗?

B: 可以。谢谢你。

会话 B

A: I would like to make a long-distance call to California, please.

B: Person-to-person or station-to-station?

A: Station-to-station.

B: What's the number, please?

A: Area code 415, 789-0277.

B: One moment, please.

A: Thank you.

A: 我想打一个长途电话到加利福尼亚州。

B: 叫人的或叫号的?

A: 叫号的。

B: 请问电话号码是什么?

A: 区号为 415,对方电话是 789-0277。

B: 请稍候。

A: 谢谢。

2 *Vocabulary & Idioms* 单词短语注解

会话 A

1. **Dr.** [ˈdɑktə] 名 医生，医师（为 doctor 的缩写）

2. **clinic** [ˈklɪnɪk] 名 诊所

3. **help** [hɛlp] 动 帮忙，帮助

4. **I'd like to** + 动词原形　我想要……（I'd like 为 I would like 的缩写）

5. **make an appointment** 约定，安排约会
   make [mek] 动 做，安排
   appointment [əˈpɔɪntmənt] 名 约定，约会

6. **Micky** [ˈmɪkɪ] 名 米奇（男性名）

7. **in the afternoon** 下午，午后
   afternoon [ˌæftəˈnun] 名 下午，午后

8. **OK** [ˌoˈke] 形 好；可以的
   = okay

会话 B

1. **long-distance** [lɔŋˈdɪstəns] 形 长途的
   long [lɔŋ] 形（长度、距离、时间等）长的
   distance [ˈdɪstəns] 名 距离
   long-distance call 长途电话

2. **California** [ˌkæləˈfɔrnjə] 名 加利福尼亚州（位于美国西海岸）

3. **person-to-person** [ˈpɝsn̩ˌtuˈpɝsn̩] 形 叫人的（电话用语）
   person [ˈpɝsn̩] 名 人

4. **station-to-station** [ˈsteʃənˌtuˈsteʃən] 形 叫号的（电话用语）
   station [ˈsteʃən] 名 局

5. **number** [ˈnʌmbə] 名 号码

6. **area code** 区域码，区号

area [`ɛrɪə] 名 地区
code [kod] 名 代号

3 ***Grammar Points*** 语法重点 〜〜

会话 A

1. **Hello, Dr. Chen's clinic.** 你好，我们这里是陈医生诊所。
   = Hello, this is Dr. Chen's clinic.
   a. 电话铃声响起，拿起听筒，欲表示"我 / 我们这里是某公司 / 场所"时，应使用下列句型：

   Hello, this is + 公司 / 组织名称

   例 Hello, this is Johnson Health Center. May I help you?
   你好，我们这里是约翰逊健身中心。我可以帮您什么忙吗？
   不可说：

   Hello, we are Johnson Health Center. (×)
   b. 上述句型中"this is"可予省略，故：

   Hello, this is Dr. Chen's clinic. May I help you?
   = Hello, Dr. Chen's clinic. May I help you?

   Hello, this is Johnson Health Center. May I help you?
   = Hello, Johnson Health Center. May I help you?

2. **May I help you?** 我可以帮您什么忙吗？
   本问句是个礼貌的问句，除可用于电话应对外，尚可用于商店内的对话中。
   咱们中国人进入商店或百货公司时，店员常会说："请问您要买什么？"，直译成英文则为：
   What do you want to buy, please?
   不过这样的问句在英美人士听起来是不礼貌的。在他们的国度里，店员都会采用下列礼貌问句：
   May I help you?
   Can I help you?
   Can I be of any service to you?

* service [ˈsɜvɪs] 名 服务

What can I do for you?

以上各句均可译成"我可以帮您什么忙吗？"、"我可以为你效劳吗？"。

例 A: May I help you?

B: Yes，I'm looking for a pen for my husband.

A: This way，please.

A: 我可以帮您什么忙吗？

B: 可以，我正要为我先生选购一支笔。

A: 请跟我来。

  * look for... 寻找……

  * husband [ˈhʌzbənd] 名 丈夫

例 A: What can I do for you? 我可以为您效劳吗？

B: I'm just looking around. 我只是随便瞧瞧。

A: Take your time，sir. 先生，您慢慢儿来。

3. **I'd like to make an appointment to see Dr. Chen.**

= I would like to make an appointment to see Dr. Chen.

我想约见陈医生。

注意"I would like to..."与"I like to..."的不同：

a.　I would like to + 动词原形　我想要……

例 I'd like to go to the movies tonight. 今晚我想去看电影。

I would like to sing a song for you. 我想为你唱一首歌。

b.　I like to + 动词原形　我喜欢……

例 I like to go to the movies. 我喜欢看电影。

I like to sing. 我喜欢唱歌。

c.　比较"I'd like to..."与"I want to..."的不同：

I'd like to... 我想要……

I want to... 我要……

以上两个句型均表示说话者的意愿，但"I'd like to..."语气较为委婉客气，而"I want to..."则语气较直接。

例 I'd like to see you tonight. 我今晚想跟你见面。

I want to see you tonight. 我今晚要跟你见面。

4. **Is 4 o'clock in the afternoon OK?** 下午 4 点钟可以吗?

本问句采用了下列句型:

Is... \|OK / fine / all right\| (with you)? ……（对你）可以吗?

例 A: Can you come today? 你今天能来吗?

B: Sorry, I can't. I'm very busy. 抱歉,我不能。我很忙。

A: Then, is tomorrow fine with you? 那么,你明天可以吗?

B: Yes, it is. 可以。

会话 B

本会话旨在介绍通过总机小姐或先生(均称为 operator [ˈɑpəˌretə])打国际长途电话时的一些用语。今天许多国家的电话系统已采用国际直拨系统(即 the International Direct Dialing System, 简称 IDD),也就是我们可直接在电话上拨号码便可与我们想要联络的人直接通话。但出国旅游或在某些情况下,我们得借助电话机为我们联络,故下列这些实用的用语我们应牢记:

1. **make a call** 打一个电话

= make a telephone call

= make a phone call

例 I'd like to make a long-distance call to New York, please.
我想打一个长途电话到纽约。

2. **Person-to-person or station-to-station?**

叫人的还是叫号的?

本问句系由下列问句简化而成:

Is it a person-to-person call or a station-to-station call?

这是一个叫人的电话还是叫号的电话?

我们通过总机打长途电话时,若指定要某人接电话,这时就称作"a person-to-person call"(叫人的电话);若不指定某人接电话,即任何人接电话都可以,这时就称作"a station-to-station call"(叫号的电话)。

3. **Area code 415, 789-0277.**

区域码 / 区号为 415，对方电话是 789-0277。

area code 区域码 / 区号（指对方住的省份或城市代号）

country code 国际区号，国码

欲从中国打直拨电话给美国加利福尼亚州旧金山的友人，就须拨
下列号码：

$\underline{86}$	$\underline{1}$
中国国际区号	美国国际区号
415	625-3071
加利福尼亚州旧金山区域码	友人电话号码

④   *Substitution* 替换

1. Hello, Dr. Chen's | clinic.
                      | office.   哈啰，这里是陈医生诊所。

   = Hello, this is Dr. Chen's | clinic.
                               | office.

2. May | I help you? 我可以帮您什么忙吗？
   Can |

   = What can I do for you?

3. I'd like to | make an appointment to see Dr. Chen. 我想约见陈医生。
              | have a cup of tea. 我想要喝杯茶。
              | go with you. 我想要跟你去。

4. Is 4 o'clock in the afternoon | OK?
                                     | fine?   下午 4 点钟可以吗？
                                     | all right?

5. I would like to | make | a long-distance call to California, please.
                     | place |
   我想打一个长途电话到加利福尼亚州。

⑤ **Exercises** 练习　　　　　　　　　　 C*

I. Use the right word: 请选出适当的单词：

with	this✓	do✓	service
to	place	would	code

1. Hello, _this_ is Dr. Ho's clinic.
2. What can I _do_ for you?
3. I'd like to _make_ a long-distance call.
4. I _would_ like to go home now.
5. Is this afternoon OK _with_ you?
6. I'd like to make a long-distance call _to_ Mr. Li.
7. What's the area _code_ , please?
8. Can I be of any _service_ to you?

II. Complete the dialogue: 完成下列会话：

A: Hello, Dr. Ho's office. M _ay_ I help you?

B: I'd like to m _ake_ an appointment to see Dr. Ho.

A: What's your n _ame_ , please?

B: This is Mrs. Wang.

A: Is 3 o'clock this afternoon a _ll_ r _ight_ with you?

B: Not really. I would l _ike_ to come at 2 o'clock.

A: OK. That's f _ine_ .

B: T _hank_ you. Bye.

Lesson 11

Telephone Conversation III
电话会话(三)

1 **Dialogue** 会话

会话 A

A: Hello, room service.

B: This is room 369. I'd like to order some food, please.

A: I'm sorry, but the kitchen's closed.

B: What do you have?

A: We have only sandwiches and drinks.

B: That'll be fine. I'm starving.

A: 你好，这里是客房服务中心。

B: 这里是 369 号房。我想要点菜。

A: 很抱歉，厨房已经关闭了。

B: 那你们有什么?

A: 我们只有三明治和饮料。

B: 那也可以。我饿坏了。

会话 B

A: Hello, front desk. Can I help you?

B: Can you give me a morning call, please?

A: Sure. What time do you want to get up?

B: Please call me at 6:00 a.m.

A: No problem.

B: Thank you.

A: 你好, 这里是前台。我可以为您效劳吗?

B: 可不可以请你在早上打电话叫我起床?

A: 当然。您想什么时候起床呢?

B: 请在早上6点钟打电话叫我。

A: 没问题。

B: 谢谢。

② *Vocabulary & Idioms* 单词短语注解

会话 A

1. **room service** （饭店内的）客房服务（中心）   *be at your service*
   room [rum]名 房间；service [ˈsɝvɪs]名 服务

2. **order** [ˈɔrdɚ]动 点（餐）；订购

3. **some** [sʌm]形 一些，若干

4. **food** [fud]名 食物

5. **kitchen** [ˈkɪtʃɪn]名 厨房

6. **closed** [klozd]形 （尤指商店或公共场所等）停止营业的，关闭的

7. **only** [ˈonlɪ]副 仅，只

8. **sandwich** [ˈsændwɪtʃ]名 三明治

9. **drink** [drɪŋk]名 饮料

10. **starve** [stɑrv]动 饥饿；饿死（starving 是 starve 的现在分词）

会话 B

1. **front desk** （饭店中的）前台
   front [frʌnt]形 前面的；desk [dɛsk]名 办公桌；书桌

2. **morning call** 早上叫人起床的电话

3. **get up** 起床

4. **No problem.** 没问题。problem [ˈprɑbləm]名 问题

③ *Grammar Points* 语法重点

会话 A

1. **Hello, room service.** 你好，这里是客房服务中心。
   本句之原句法为：
   Hello, this is the room service department / section.

* section [ˈsɛkʃən]名 区（域）；部门

但实际使用时，只说 room service，而不说 the room service department
或 the room service section。

room service 是饭店中的客房服务中心，供房客叫餐饮、点心之类
的地方。有些房客不在餐厅中用餐，这时就可通过 room service 的
服务将餐点送至房间。

例 A: Hello, room service. 你好，这里是客房服务中心。

B: This is room 301. I'd like to order some drinks, please.
这里是 301 号房。我想要点些饮料。

A: Sure. What would you like? 好的。您想要点什么？

2. **I'd like to order some food, please.** 我想点一些菜。

a. order 可表"点（餐）"或"订购"之意。

例 I'll order a pizza for dinner tonight. 我今晚要叫个比萨当晚餐。

If the bookstore doesn't have this book, they can order it for
you.

如果那家书店没有这本书，他们可以为你订购。

b. 在餐厅中，服务人员欲向客人点菜时，常使用下列问句：

Are you ready to order, sir?

先生，您是不是准备好要点菜了呢？

May I take your order now? 我可不可以接受您的点菜呢？

例 A: May I take your order now? 我可不可以接受您的点菜呢？

B: I'm not ready to order yet. Please give me a minute.
我还没准备好要点餐。请再给我一点时间。

c. order 也可表"命令"的意思，句型如下：

order ＋人＋to＋动词　命令某人做……

例 You don't have the right to order me to do things for you.
你没有权利命令我为你做事。

3. **I'm sorry, but the kitchen's closed.** 很抱歉，厨房已经关闭了。

a. 表示"很抱歉／对不起……"的"I'm sorry, but..."及"Excuse
me, but..."之重要用法我们已在 Lesson 2 会话 A 中提过，因此
不再多加赘述，但由于这是很实用的句型，所以此处再提供例

句供读者参考，希望读者能更熟悉这两种用法的不同。

例 I'm sorry, but you are wrong. 很抱歉，你错了。

I'm sorry, but I must leave now. 很抱歉，我现在必须离开了。

Excuse me, but where is the post office?

打扰一下，请问邮局在哪儿？

Excuse me, but do you have the time?

打扰一下，请问现在几点钟？

b. 本句中的 closed 是形容词，用来表示餐厅、商店、公司等"停止营业的"、"不开放的"或"关闭的"，而动词 close 则可用来表示餐厅、商店、公司等"打烊"、"停止营业"、"关闭"等。

例 The museum is closed on Mondays.

那间博物馆每星期一都不开放。

* museum [mjuˈzɪəm] 名 博物馆

The bookstore closes at 10:00 p.m. every day.

那家书店每天晚上 10 点打烊。

c. close 也可用来表示一般的"关闭"，如：close the door（关门）、close the window（关窗户）等。

例 Please close the window. It's cold. 请关上窗户。天气很冷。

4. **That'll be fine.** 那也可以。

例 A: Do you have any coffee? 你们有什么咖啡吗？

B: No. But we have tea. 没有。不过我们有茶。

A: That'll be fine. 那也可以。

5. **I'm starving.** 我饿坏了。

上句中的 starving 是动词 starve 的现在分词，starve 是"饥饿"或"挨饿"的意思，"I'm starving."就是指"我饿坏了。"也就等于"I am very hungry."。

例 I'm starving. Do you have anything to eat?

我饿坏了。你有什么东西可以吃吗？

甚至还有下列夸张的说法：

I'm starving to death. 我快饿死了。

* death [dεθ] 名 死（亡）

会话 B

1. **Hello, front desk.** 你好，这里是前台。

   front desk 的字面意思直译为"前面的桌子"，但我们可千万不能这样翻译，front desk 的真正意思指的是"饭店中的前台"。我们现在来介绍有关 front 的一个重要的用法：

   in front of... 在……的前面

   例 There's a department store in front of the train station.
   火车站前面有一家百货公司。

2. **Can you give me a morning call, please?**
   可不可以请你在早上打电话给我叫我起床？

   morning call 特指在早上叫人起床的电话，而 wake-up call 也是指叫人起床的电话，但是不限于在什么时间。

   例 Can you give me a morning call at 5 tomorrow, please?
   可不可以请你在明早 5 点钟打电话给我叫我起床？

   Can you give me a wake-up call at 4 p.m., please?
   可不可以请你在下午 4 点钟打电话给我叫我起床？

3. **get up** 起床

   go to bed 上床睡觉

   例 I usually go to bed at 10 p.m. and get up at 6 in the morning every day.
   我每天通常在晚上 10 点钟就寝，早上 6 点钟起床。

4. **Please call me at 6:00 a.m.** 请在早上 6 点钟打电话叫我。

   = Please give me a call at 6:00 a.m.

   = Please ring me (up) at 6:00 a.m.

   = Please give me a ring at 6:00 a.m.

   欲表"打电话给某人"可采用下列短语：

   call + 人（美式用法）

   = give + 人 + a call（美式用法）

   = ring + 人（up）（英式用法）

   = give + 人 + a ring（英式用法）

例 I'll
| call you
| give you a call
| ring you (up)
| give you a ring
tonight. 今晚我会打电话给你。

5. **No problem.** 没问题。

这是一种用来响应他人、表示愿意做对方所要求之事或有能力做某事的用语。

例 A: Can you lend me 100 dollars? 你可以借我 100 块钱吗？

B: No problem. 没问题。

A: Can you do the job? 你会做这个工作吗？

B: No problem. 没问题。

4 ### Substitution 替换

1. I'd like to order | some food, | please. | 我想点一些菜。
   | two steaks, | | 我想点两客牛排。
   | a cup of coffee, | | 我想点一杯咖啡。

2. I'm sorry, but | the kitchen's closed. | 很抱歉，厨房已经关闭了。
   | I can't go with you. | 很抱歉，我不能和你一起去。
   | you must leave now. | 很抱歉，你现在必须要离开了。

3. I'm | starving. | 我饿坏了。
   | very hungry.

4. Can you give me a | morning call, | please?
   | wake-up call, |
   可不可以请你在早上打电话给我叫我起床？
   可不可以请你打电话给我叫我起床？

5. Please | call me at 6:00 a.m. 请在早上 6 点钟打电话叫我。
   | give me a call tomorrow. 明天请打个电话给我。
   | ring me (up) as soon as possible. 请尽快打电话给我。

5 ### Exercises 练习

I. Use the right word: 请选出适当的单词：

closed	close	but	front
take	order	ready	get

1. I'd like to _order_ some milk, please.
2. Are you _ready_ to order, sir?
3. Can I _take_ your order now?
4. The restaurant's _closed_.
5. I'm sorry, _but_ we don't have ice cream.
6. Please _close_ the door when you leave.
7. There's a bookstore in _front_ of my school.
8. I _get_ up early every morning.

II. Complete the dialogue: 完成下列会话 :

    A: Hello, front desk. Can I h_elp_____ you?

    B: I want to g_et_____ up at 7 a.m. tomorrow morning.

    A: Yes?

    B: Can you give me a m_orning_ c _all___ , please?

    A: Sure. What's your r_oom__ number?

    B: It's 707.

    A: OK. I'll call a _tound_/_ot_ 7 a.m.

    B: Thank you.

    A: No p_roblem_.

Lesson 12

Buying Things
买东西

会话 A

A: How much does that pen cost?

B: It costs ten dollars.

A: That's very expensive. Do you have anything cheaper?

B: Sure. This pen is only two dollars.

A: Good. I'll take it.

A: 那支笔要多少钱?

B: 10 块钱。

A: 那很贵。你们有没有比较便宜的?

B: 当然。这支笔只要两块钱。

A: 好。我就买这支。

会话 B

A: How much is this book?

B: It's seven dollars.

A: Do you have change for a hundred?

B: No problem.

A: OK. Here's the money.

B: Thank you. Here's the book and your change.

A: 这本书要多少钱?

B: 7 块钱。

A: 你有零钱找开 100 块吗?

B: 没问题。

A: 好。钱给你。

B: 谢谢。这儿是您的书和零钱。

2　*Vocabulary & Idioms* 单词短语注解　✎

会话 A

1. **buy** [baɪ] 动（购）买

2. **thing** [θɪŋ] 名 东西

3. **how much** 多少价格
   much [mʌtʃ] 代 大量

4. **pen** [pɛn] 名 笔（可指钢笔或圆珠笔）

5. **cost** [kɔst] 动 价值（若干），需花（多少钱）

6. **dollar** [ˈdɑləˌ] 名 元，美元

7. **expensive** [ɪkˈspɛnsɪv] 形 昂贵的

8. **anything** [ˈɛnɪˌθɪŋ] 代 任何东西

9. **cheaper** [ˈtʃipəˌ] 形 比较便宜的（cheaper 是 cheap 的比较级）
   cheap [tʃip] 形 便宜的

会话 B

1. **book** [bʊk] 名 书（籍）

2. **change** [tʃendʒ] 名 零钱

3. **money** [ˈmʌnɪ] 名（金）钱

3　*Grammar Points* 语法重点　〰

会话 A

1. **How much does that pen cost?** 那支笔要花多少钱？

   = How much is that pen? 那支笔多少钱？

   我们想表示"某物品要（花）多少钱？"时，可用下列句型：

   How much (money) | does + 单数物品 | cost?
   　　　　　　　　　| do + 复数物品 |

$$= \text{How much (money)} \begin{vmatrix} \text{is} + \text{单数物品} \\ \text{are} + \text{复数物品} \end{vmatrix} ?$$

例 How much money does that shirt cost? 那件衬衫要多少钱?

= How much does that shirt cost?

= How much money is that shirt?

= How much is that shirt?

How much (money) do these pencils cost? 这些铅笔要多少钱?

= How much (money) are these pencils?

a. 上列句型中的 much 为代词, how much 理论上是由 how much money 简化而来 (money 通常不须说出, 以免造成赘述), 此时的 much 则是形容词, 专门用来修饰不可数名词。初学英文者可能搞不清楚什么是可数名词和不可数名词, 我们现在先以 money (金钱) 为例来说明什么是不可数名词 : money 是不可数名词, 但这并非指 "钱" 不能数, "钱" 当然可以数, 如 : 1 美元 (one dollar)、两毛钱 (two dimes)、3 分钱 (three cents) 等 ; 所谓 "不可数" 乃指 money 这个单词本身不能数, 我们不能说 "1 个钱" (one money)、"两个钱" (two moneys), 亦即 money 这个词没有复数形式。

例 中文 : 你有多少钱?

英文 : How many moneys do you have? (×)

→ How much money do you have? (√)

我们再以 paper (纸) 为例

我们不能说 "一纸" (a paper)、"两纸" (two papers), 但可以说 "一张纸"、"两张纸", 这时就要加上表示 "张" 的单位

a sheet of paper piece, 即 "a piece of paper"、"two pieces of paper"。

water (水) 也是不可数名词, 我们不能说 "一水" (a water)、"两水" (two waters), 但若加上单位, 如 "一杯"、"两杯" 等, 这时就可以说 "一杯水" (a glass of water)、"两杯水" (two glasses of water)。

a cup of coffee

b. 所谓可数名词就是该单词本身可以数, 像 book (书)、student (学生) 等, 可以说 one book / student (一本书 / 一个学生), two books / students (两本书 / 两个学生), 这时就不能用 much 修

饰，而要用 many。

例 How much books do you have? (×)

→ How many books do you have? (√)

你有多少本书？

How much students are there in the room? (×)

→ How many students are there in the room? (√)

房间里有多少个学生？

There are five books in the bag. 袋子里有 5 本书。

There are fifty students in the classroom. 教室里有 50 个学生。

c. 上列句型中的 cost 表"价值(多少钱)"，使用这个词时，不可以"人"作主语，因为如果我们说：

Sb. spend(s) money

John costs ten dollars. 约翰价值 10 块钱。

这句话的意思是说只要花 10 块钱就可以买到约翰，我想是没有人会想要这么做的。因此，使用 cost 时，通常都以"物品"、"东西"等作主语，表示某物品／东西"价值若干"。

例 The dress costs twenty dollars. 那件衣服要 20 块钱。

我们也可以在 cost 之后接"人"，再加金钱，表示"花某人多少钱"的意思。

例 This hat may cost her thirty dollars.

这顶帽子可能会花她 30 块钱。

2. **That's very expensive.** 那很贵。

a. expensive 是形容词，表示"(价格)昂贵的"，多用来修饰物品，而不可以用来修饰价钱(price [praɪs])。

例 The price of the car is expensive. (×)

→ The car is expensive. (√)

这部车很贵。

b. 价钱的昂贵或便宜可以用 high(高)或 low(低)来表示。

例 The price of the house is expensive. (×)

→ The price of the house is high. (√)

这栋房子的价格很高。

The house is expensive. 这栋房子很贵。

Eggs are selling at a low price. 鸡蛋现在售价很低。

3. **Do you have <u>anything cheaper</u>?** 你们有没有比较便宜的东西？

a. 上列句中的 anything 表"任何事物"的意思，与 something（某事，某物）及 nothing（无事，无物）均为代词，可用来代替事情或物品。anything <u>使用于否定句及疑问句中，而 something 则</u>使用于肯定句中；nothing 因本身具否定意味，因此不可再与否定词（如 not、no 等）连用，以避免形成双重否定。

使用这三个词时要注意的是：

形容词修饰一般名词时，通常置于该名词前。但形容词修饰 anything、something 及 nothing 时，该形容词要置于这三个代词之后，而不可置于其前。

例 Do you have <u>important anything</u> to tell me? (×)

→ Do you have <u>anything important</u> to tell me? (√)

你有什么重要的事情要告诉我吗？

I don't have <u>anything important</u> to tell you.

我没有什么重要的事情要告诉你。

I have <u>something good</u> for you.

我有好东西给你。

The poor man <u>doesn't</u> have <u>nothing</u> to eat. (×)

→ The poor man <u>has nothing</u> to eat. (√)

= The poor man <u>doesn't</u> have <u>anything</u> to eat.

那可怜的男子没有东西可吃。

There's <u>nothing nice</u> to eat in that restaurant.

= There <u>isn't anything nice</u> to eat in that restaurant.

那家餐厅没什么好吃的东西。

b. 上列句中的 cheaper（比较便宜的）是形容词 cheap（便宜的）的比较级。

一般而言，原级是双音节或三音节以上的形容词，变成比较级的方法是在其前加 more，如：

	原级		比较级
	expensive（昂贵的）	→	more expensive（比较贵的）
	important（重要的）	→	more important（比较重要的）
	beautiful（漂亮的）	→	more beautiful（比较漂亮的）

而原级是单音节的形容词变成比较级的方法则是在字尾加 -er。

如：

	原级		比较级
	cheap（便宜的）	→	cheaper（比较便宜的）
	tall（高的）	→	taller（比较高的）
	cold（冷的）	→	colder（比较冷的）

原级是以辅音结尾的单音节形容词变成比较级时，则是要先重复该辅音字母，再加 -er，如：

	原级		比较级
	hot（热的）	→	hotter（比较热的）
	fat（肥胖的）	→	fatter（比较胖的）

有关上述形容词比较级的变化只是个粗略的介绍，对初学英文的我们，在现阶段并不须要太钻研，随着文章愈看愈多自然就会愈来愈了解这些用法，因为学英文是需要耐心和时间的。

4. **I'll take it.** 我就把它买下了。

这是在商店中常用的会话，表示要买下某个东西之意，就等于"I'll buy it."。

例 A: This book is very good. You should buy it.

B: All right. I'll $\begin{vmatrix} \text{take} \\ \text{buy} \end{vmatrix}$ it.

A: 这本书很好，你应该买下它。

B: 好，那我就把它买下了。

会话 B

1. **Do you have <u>change</u> for a hundred?** 你有零钱找开 100 块吗？

= Do you have change for a hundred dollars?

上列句中的 change（零钱）是不可数名词，我们不能说"一个零钱"

（a change）、"两个零钱"（two changes）等。同理, cash（现金）亦是不可数名词, 我们也不能说"一个现金"（a cash）、"两个现金"（two cashes）等。

例 中文：你需要多少零钱?

　　英文：How many changes do you need? (×)

　　→ How much change do you need? (√)

例 A: How much change do you have? 你有多少零钱?

　　= How much do you have in change?

　　B: I have change for ten dollars. 我有 10 块零钱。

　　= I have ten dollars in change.

　　A: How much cash do you have? 你有多少现金?

　　= How much do you have in cash?

　　B: I have cash for one hundred. 我有 100 块现金。

　　= I have one hundred in cash.

2. **OK. Here's the money.** 好。钱给你。

我们要拿东西给别人时, 常可使用下列句型:

Here is / Here's + 单数名词

Here are / Here're + 复数名词

上列句型可译为"……给你"或"……在这儿"。

例 A: That will be fifty dollars, please. 那要 50 块钱。

　　B: Here's a hundred. 给你 100 块。

　　A: Here is the money. 给你钱。

　　B: Here're the books. 这儿是你要的书。

但更常用的一句话是"Here you are."（或"Here you go."）, 表"你要的东西在这里"、"拿去吧"或"在这儿"的意思。

例 A: Can I have a look at that shirt? 我可以看一下那件衬衫吗?

　　B: Here you are. 给你。

　　= Here you go.

4 Substitution 替换

1. How much | does that pen cost? / is that pen? 那支钢笔要多少钱？ *brush 毛笔*

2. It costs / It's | ten dollars. 它价值 / 要 10 块钱。

3. That's very | expensive. / cheap. 那很贵 / 便宜。

4. Do you have anything | cheaper? / special? 你们有没有比较便宜的 / 特别的？

5. I'll | take / buy | it. 我就把它买下了。

6. Here's | the money. 给你钱。 / the book. 书在这儿。

7. Here you | are. / go. 拿去吧 / 在这儿。

5 Exercises 练习

I. Use the right word: 请选出适当的单词：

| are | much | change | high |
| many | is | take | something |

1. How _much_ does this book cost?
2. How _many_ students do you have?
3. There _are_ many schools in the city.
4. There _is_ a pretty girl waiting for you.
5. I won't buy that car; the price is too _high_.
6. I have _something_ exciting to tell you.
7. Do you have _change_ for a thousand dollars?
8. This tie isn't expensive. I'll _take_ it.

II. Complete the dialogue: 完成下列会话 :

A: How m_uch_ is this shirt?

B: It c_osts_ sixty dollars.

A: It's expensive. Do you have anything c_heaper_

B: Sure. These are only twenty dollars.

A: The p_rice_ is OK. I'll b_uy_ two.

B: Good. H_ere_ are the shirts.

A: Do you have change f_or_ a hundred dollars?

B: Sure. Here's your change.

Lesson 13

At the Restaurant
在餐厅

会话 A

A: Do you have a table for two?

B: Yes. In the smoking or non-smoking section?

A: Non-smoking, please.

B: OK. This way, please.

A: May I have the menu?

B: Sure. Here you are.

A: 你们有两个人坐的餐桌吗？

B: 有的。您是要在吸烟区或非吸烟区？

A: 麻烦在非吸烟区。

B: 好的。请跟我这边走。

A: 可以给我菜单吗？

B: 当然。给你。

会话 B

A: May I take your order now?

B: Yes, please. I'll have the steak.

A: How would you like it?

B: Well-done, please.

A: Would you like some dessert?

B: No, thank you.

A: How about something to drink?

B: Hot coffee, please.

A: 我可以接受您的点菜了吗？

B: 是的，麻烦你。我要牛排。

A: 您的牛排要几分熟？

B: 麻烦要全熟。

A: 您要不要来些甜点呢？

B: 不用了，谢谢。

A: 那您要不要喝点什么呢？

B: 麻烦要热咖啡。

2 Vocabulary & Idioms 单词短语注解

会话 A

1. **restaurant** [ˈrɛstərənt] 名 餐厅

2. **table** [ˈtebḷ] 名 桌子

3. **smoking section** 吸烟区
   non-smoking section 非吸烟区，禁烟区
   smoking [ˈsmokɪŋ] 形 吸烟的
   non-smoking [nɑnˈsmokɪŋ] 形 禁烟的
   section [ˈsɛkʃən] 名 区（域）

4. **or** [ɔr] 连 或，或者

5. **way** [we] 名 方向

6. **menu** [ˈmɛnju] 名 菜单

会话 B

1. **order** [ˈɔrdɚ] 名 & 动 点（餐）

2. **steak** [stek] 名 牛排

3. **well-done** [ˌwɛlˈdʌn] 形 （食物）煮透的，完全熟透的

4. **dessert** [dɪˈzɝt] 名 餐后甜点，点心

5. **something** [ˈsʌmθɪŋ] 代 某物；某事

6. **drink** [drɪŋk] 动 喝 & 名 饮料

7. **coffee** [ˈkɔfɪ] 名 咖啡

3 Grammar Points 语法重点

会话 A

　　本课主要介绍一些在餐厅用餐时常用的会话，希望读者能够熟悉这些用语。

1. **Do you have a table for two?** 你们有两个人坐的餐桌吗？

   = Do you have a table for two people?

   "a table for + 数字"是指"供……（人）坐的餐桌"，是在餐厅用餐时很实用的句型，因为在一般较高级的餐厅用餐时，是不可以直接到餐桌去坐，而要先在餐厅门口的等候区等服务人员带位。

   例 A: Do you have a table for ten? 你们有 10 个人坐的餐桌吗？

   B: Sure. This way, please. 当然有。请跟我这边走。

   用电话预约餐桌时，则可使用下列句型：

   例 A: Hello, Lai-lai Restaurant. May I help you?

   B: Yes. I'd like to book a table for seven.

   = Yes. I'd like to reserve a table for seven.

   A: 你好，来来餐厅。我可以帮您什么忙吗？

   B: 是的，我想订一张七个人的餐桌。

   * book [buk] 动 预订（座位等）

   reserve [rɪˈzɝv] 动 预订（座位、门票等）

2. **Yes. In the smoking or non-smoking section?**

   有的。您是要在吸烟区或非吸烟区？

   本句是由"Yes. Do you want a table in the smoking section or in the non-smoking section?"简化而来的。

   目前在一般的公共场所都有划分吸烟区和非吸烟区，这是因为现代人的健康意识高涨，而二手烟有害身体健康，故有此区别；而有些场所，像飞机上、车站内等甚至还有全面禁烟的规定。

   例 A: Can I have a window seat, please?

   B: Yes. In the smoking or non-smoking section?

   A: 麻烦可以给我靠窗的座位吗？

   B: 好的。您是要在吸烟区或非吸烟区？

3. **This way, please.** 请跟我这边走。

   本句原为"Follow me (in) this way, please."，但因为经常使用，故简化为"This way, please."。

   follow [ˈfɑlo] 动 跟随

   (in) this way 朝这边

注意

一般使用时, in this way 中的 in 经常可予以省略, 而简化为 this way。

例 A: Do you have any French books? 你们有什么法文书籍吗?

B: This way, please. 请跟我这边走。

会话 B

1. **May I take your order now?** 我可以接受您的点菜了吗?

餐厅的服务人员欲向用餐的客人点菜时, 通常有下列说法:

May I take your order now?(order 是名词)

我可以接受您的点菜了吗?

Are you ready to order now, sir / ma'am?(order 是动词)

先生 / 女士, 您现在准备要点菜了吗?

Would you like to order now, sir / ma'am?(order 是动词)

先生 / 女士, 您现在想要点菜了吗?

上列第二个及第三个用法中的 sir 及 ma'am 分别表示"先生"、"女士", sir 是对男性的尊称, ma'am 则是对女性的尊称。

例 Waiter: May I take your order now?

Customer: Yes, please. I'll have the chicken rice, please.

侍者: 我可以接受您的点菜了吗?

顾客: 是的, 麻烦你。请给我来份鸡肉饭。

* waiter [ˈwetɚ] 名 (餐厅的) 男侍者 / 服务生

* customer [ˈkʌstəmɚ] 名 顾客

Waitress: Are you ready to order now, sir / ma'am?

Customer: Can I have another minute, please?

女侍者: 先生 / 女士, 您现在准备要点菜了吗?

顾 客: 请再等我一下。

* waitress [ˈwetrɪs] 名 (餐厅的) 女侍者 / 服务生

2. **How would you like it?** 您的牛排要几分熟?

= How would you like your steak?

本句中的 it 为代词, 代替上一句中已提过的名词 steak。我们想询问某人的食物要如何调理时，可使用下列句型：

How would you like your + 食物名称?

您的……（食物）要如何调理？

例 A: How would you like your steak? 你的牛排要几分熟？

B: I'd like it well-done / medium / medium rare / rare.

我要全熟 / 六七分熟 / 四五分熟 / 三分熟。

* medium [ˈmidɪəm] 形（牛排）煎成中等嫩度的

rare [rɛr] 形（肉）半熟的，未完全煮熟的

A: How would you like your coffee? 你的咖啡要怎么泡？

B: Black, please.

Just sugar, please.

Cream and no sugar, please.

With sugar and cream, please.

麻烦什么都不加（即清咖啡）/ 只加糖 / 加奶精不要加糖 / 糖与奶精都要。

3. **No, thank you.** 不用了，谢谢。

当有人询问你需不需要什么东西或任何帮忙、服务时，表"要"与"不要"通常用下列说法来表示：

表"（需）要"时：

Yes, please. 是的 / 好，麻烦你。

表"不（需）要"时：

No, |thank you. 不用了，谢谢。
    |thanks.

例 A: Would you like some coffee? 你要来点咖啡吗？

B: Yes, please. / No, thank you. |好，麻烦你。
                                 |不用了，谢谢。

A: Would you want me to carry your bags? 要我帮你拿袋子吗？

B: Yes, please. / No, thanks. |好啊，麻烦你。
                              |不用了，多谢。

4. **How about something to drink?** 要不要喝点什么呢？

= Would you like something to drink?

a. How about + 名词? 要不要来点……呢?

= Would you like + 名词?

How about + 动名词? 要不要……呢 /……怎么样呢?

= Would you like to + 动词原形?

例 How about a cup of tea? 要不要来杯茶呢?

= Would you like a cup of tea?

How about going to a movie tonight?

= Would you like to go to a movie tonight?

今晚要不要去看场电影呀?

b. 在上一课中，我们已提过 something、anything 及 nothing 等三个代词与形容词连用时，形容词要放在这三个代词之后；但 something、anything 及 nothing 之后亦可接不定式短语 (即 "to + 动词原形")，此时的不定式短语也作形容词用，修饰其前的 something、anything 或 nothing。

例 I am hungry. I need something to eat.

我饿了。我需要吃点东西。

* to eat 修饰 something。

Don't you have anything to do? 你难道没什么事好做吗?

* to do 修饰 anything。

I have nothing to tell you. 我没什么事要告诉你。

* to tell you 修饰 nothing。

4 Substitution 替换

1. Do you have a table for | two? | 你们有两个人 / 六个人坐的餐桌吗?
   | six? |

2. May I have the | menu? | 可以给我菜单 / 账单吗?
   | check / bill? |

   * check [tʃɛk] 名 账单；bill [bɪl] 名 账单

3. | May I take your order now? | 我可以接受您的点菜了吗?
   | Are you ready to order now? | 您现在准备要点菜了吗?
   | Would you like to order now? | 您现在想要点菜了吗?

4. How would you like your | steak? | 你的牛排要几分熟?
   | eggs? | 你的蛋要怎么煮?

5. How about | something to drink? 要不要喝点什么呢?
   | going on a picnic tomorrow? 明天去野餐怎么样呀?

   * picnic [ˈpɪknɪk] 名 野餐

5 Exercises 练习

I. Use the right word: 请选出适当的单词:

anything	book	take	about
to	like	for	nothing

1. Do you have a table _____ four, please?
2. I'd like to _____ a ticket to France, please.
3. May I _____ your order now?
4. How would you _____ your steak?
5. Don't you have _____ to wear?
6. How _____ some music?
7. I need something _____ read.
8. I have _____ to say to you.

II. Complete the dialogue: 完成下列会话 :

A: Would you like to o_____ now?

B: Yes, I'll have a steak.

A: How w_____ you like it?

B: Medium r_____, please.

A: Would you like anything to d_____?

B: I'll h_____ a cup of hot tea, please.

A: And would you like any d_____?

B: Yes. But can I have a look at the m_____ again, please?

Lesson 14

At the Clothing Store
在服装店

Dialogue 会话

会话 A

A: Can I have a look at that jacket, please?

B: What size do you wear?

A: Extra large.

B: Here you are.

A: Can I try it on?

B: Sure. Go ahead.

A: 请问我可以看一下那件夹克吗？

B: 你穿几号的呢？

A: 特大号的。

B: 给您。

A: 我可以试穿吗？

B: 当然。请便。

119

会话 B

A: May I help you?

B: Yes, please. I'm looking for a necktie.

A: Any special brand?

B: No. Just something simple and not too expensive.

A: How about this one?

B: That's fine. How much is it?

A: It's only US$10 and it's on sale.

B: OK. I'll take it. Thanks.

A: 我可以为您效劳吗？

B: 是的，麻烦你，我正在找一条领带。

A: 要任何特别的品牌吗？

B: 不用。只要样式简单又不太贵就可以了。

A: 这一条如何？

B: 可以。要多少钱呢？

A: 只要 10 美元，而且现在正在特价。

B: 好，我就把它买下了。谢谢。

2 Vocabulary & Idioms 单词短语注解

会话 A

1. **clothing** [ˈkloðɪŋ] 名 衣服

2. **store** [stɔr] 名 商店

3. **have a look at...** 看一看 / 瞧一瞧……
   look [lʊk] 名 & 动 看

4. **jacket** [ˈdʒækɪt] 名 夹克

5. **size** [saɪz] 名 尺寸 ;（东西的）大小

6. **wear** [wɛr] 动 穿 ; 戴

7. **extra large** 特大（号）的
   extra [ˈɛkstrə] 副 格外地，特别地
   large [lɑrdʒ] 形 大的

8. **try...on** 试穿 / 戴……（衣服、帽子等）
   try [traɪ] 动 试用 ; 尝试

会话 B

1. **necktie** [ˈnɛkˌtaɪ] 名 领带

2. **special** [ˈspɛʃəl] 形 特别的

3. **brand** [brænd] 名 品牌 ; 厂牌

4. **simple** [ˈsɪmpl] 形 简单的

5. **on sale** 减价售出，贱卖，打折
   sale [sel] 名 出售

3 Grammar Points 语法重点

标题

1. **clothing** [ˈkloðɪŋ] 名 衣服（不可数名词）

clothing 是不可数名词，虽然中文说"一件衣服"、"两件衣服"，但英文却不能说"clothing"、"two clothings"。在英文中，上衣与裤子是分开的，此时表上衣与裤子的名词才是可数名词。例如：

上衣

jacket [ˈdʒækɪt] 夹克

a jacket（一件夹克）、two jackets（两件夹克）……

coat [kot] 外套

a coat（一件外套）、two coats（两件外套）……

shirt [ʃɜt] 衬衫

a shirt（一件衬衫）、two shirts（两件衬衫）……

blouse [blaʊs] 女式衬衫 / 短上衣

a blouse（一件女衬衫）、two blouses（两件女衬衫）……

裤子

由于裤子都有两条裤管，所以表示裤子的词都用复数形式，而表"一条裤子"、"两条裤子"的单位则要用"a pair of"、"two pairs of"等来表示。

trousers [ˈtraʊzəz] 裤子

a pair of trousers（一条裤子）、two pairs of trousers（两条裤子）……

pants [pænts] 裤子

a pair of pants（一条裤子）、two pairs of pants（两条裤子）……

slacks [slæks] 休闲裤

a pair of slacks（一条休闲裤）、two pairs of slacks（两条休闲裤）……

以上不管是上衣或裤子均统称为 clothing，因为说 clothing 时搞不清楚是指上衣还是裤子，因此不说 a clothing，但我们可以说 some clothing（一些衣服）、a lot of clothing（很多衣服），因为 some、a lot of 都是可以用来修饰不可数名词的形容词。

例 She has a lot of clothing in her closet. 她的衣橱里有很多衣服。

2. **clothes** [kloz] **名** 衣服（恒用复数）

clothes 也是"衣服"的意思，但和 clothing 不同的是，clothes 始终要用复数。且 clothes 亦是不可数名词，我们除了可说 some clothes、a lot of clothes 外，还可说 many clothes，因为 many 之后

要接复数名词，所以 many clothes 是正确的，但我们不能说 many clothings，因为 clothing 无复数，但 clothing 可以用 much 来修饰。

例 I want to buy <u>some clothes</u>. 我想去买些衣服。

He has <u>many clothing</u>. (×)

→ He has <u>many clothes</u>. (√) 他有很多衣服。

He doesn't have <u>much clothing</u>. (√) 他没有很多衣服。

3. **cloth** [klɔθ] 名 布（不可数名词）

cloth（布）也是不可数名词，表"一块布"要说"a piece of cloth"、"some cloth"、"a lot of cloth"则表示"一些布"、"很多布"。

例 I always wipe the floor with an old piece of cloth.

我向来都是用旧布擦地板。

会话 A

1. **Can I have a look at that jacket, please?**

请问我可以看一下那件夹克吗?

Can I have a look at + 名词?

= Can I take a look at + 名词?

我可不可以看一看……呢?

例 A: Can I have a look at your new watch?

B: Sure. Go ahead.

A: 我可不可以看一看你的新表呢?

B: 当然可以。请吧。

Can I take a look at your new radio?

我可以看一下你的新收音机吗?

2. **What size do you wear?** 你穿几号的夹克?

= What size jacket do you wear?

a. size 本来是"尺寸"、"大小"的意思，而在这里指的就是"号码"。我们想询问别人穿几号的衣服、鞋子、帽子等时，要用 size，而不可以用 number。

例 What <u>number</u> shoes do you wear? (×)

→ What <u>size</u> shoes do you wear? (√) 你穿几号鞋?

What size socks do you wear? 你穿几号的袜子？

b. wear 代表"穿"、"戴"的意思，凡举我们身上的衣服、裤子、鞋子、帽子、皮带、眼镜、手表、项链、耳环等东西，表"穿"、"戴"的动词都可用 wear 这个词。

例 She always wears white dresses. 她总是穿白色的连衣裙。

Helen wears a hat every day. 海伦每天都戴着一顶帽子。

Tom wears a red belt to work. 汤姆系红色的皮带去上班。

He is wearing sunglasses because it's a sunny day.
因为出太阳，所以他戴着太阳眼镜。

* sunglasses [ˈsʌnˌglæsɪz] 名 太阳眼镜（因为眼镜有两个镜片，因此恒用复数）

3. **extra large** 特大号的
一般衣服、裤子等的号码可分为 small（小号）、medium（中号）、large（大号）及 extra large（特大号），这些号码通常是用大写的 S、M、L 及 XL 来表示。

例 A: What size shirt do you wear? 你穿几号的衬衫？

B: Large. 大号的。

4. **Can I try it on?** 我可以试穿吗？
try + 代词（名词）+ on / try on + 名词　试穿 / 戴……
凡是身上的衣服、裤子、帽子等物件的"试穿"、"试戴"都可用 try on 来表示。

例 Before I buy this shirt, can I try it on?
我买这件衬衫之前可以先试穿吗？

Can I try this cap on? 我可以试戴这顶帽子吗？

= Can I try on this cap?

5. **go ahead** 请便
go ahead 通常表示同意让某人（自行）做某事。

例 A: Can I use your phone? 我可以借用你的电话吗？

B: Sure. Go ahead. 当然。请便吧。

会话 B

1. **I'm looking for a necktie.** 我正在物色一条领带。

   a. 我们在 Lesson 8 中已介绍过现在进行时的用法, 这里我们再做个复习。

   现在进行时就是一种用来表示"在现在的时刻, 某动作正在进行"的状态, 相当于中文的"(现在)正在……"之意。其句型如下：

   主语 + 现在时 be 动词(is, am, are) + 现在分词……
   正在……

   例 He is <u>writing</u> a book. 他正在写一本书。

   I am <u>reading</u> the newspaper. 我正在看报纸。

   They are <u>having</u> a picnic in the park. 他们正在公园里野餐。

   b. look for... 寻找……

   例 John is looking for a new job. 约翰正在找新工作。

2. **Any special brand?** 您想要任何特别的品牌吗?

   = Do you want any special brand?

   本句 "Any special brand?" 是由 "Do you want any special brand?" 简化而来。其中的 brand 是名词, 表"厂牌"、"牌子"、"商标"的意思; brand-new 则是由 brand 衍生而来的形容词, 表"全新的"、"未用过的"之意, 也是个常用的单词。

   brand-new [ˈbrændˌnju] 名 全新的, 未用过的

   例 I like that brand of coffee most.
   我最喜欢那种牌子的咖啡。

   Be careful with that car; it's brand-new!
   请小心那辆车子;它是全新的!

3. **It's only US$10 and it's on sale.**
   那只要 10 美元, 而且现在正在特价。

   on sale 是指"减价售出"、"贱卖"或"打折"的意思, 而 for sale 则是单纯指"出售"之意。

   例 Shoes are on sale in that department store.
   那家百货公司的鞋子正在特卖。

I'm sorry, but this painting is not for sale.
很抱歉，这幅画是不卖的 / 非卖品。

4 *Substitution* 替换 ♋

1. Can I $\begin{vmatrix} \text{have} \\ \text{take} \end{vmatrix}$ a look at that jacket, please?
   请问我可以看一下那件夹克吗？

2. What size $\begin{vmatrix} \text{shirt} \\ \text{pants} \end{vmatrix}$ do you wear? 你穿几号的衬衫 / 裤子？

3. Can I $\begin{vmatrix} \text{try it on?} \\ \text{try on the watch?} \end{vmatrix}$ 我可以试穿它吗 / 试戴这块表吗？

4. I'm looking for a $\begin{vmatrix} \text{necktie.} \\ \text{wedding ring.} \end{vmatrix}$
   我正在物色一条领带 / 一枚结婚戒指。
   * wedding [ˈwɛdɪŋ] 名 婚礼
   * ring [rɪŋ] 名 戒指

5. Any special $\begin{vmatrix} \text{brand?} \\ \text{kind?} \\ \text{type?} \end{vmatrix}$ 要任何特别的品牌 / 种类 / 样式吗？

6. Just something $\begin{vmatrix} \text{simple.} \\ \text{plain.} \end{vmatrix}$ 只要样式简单就可以了。
   * plain [plen] 形 简单的，朴素的

5 *Exercises* 练习 ☪

I. Use the right word: 请选出适当的单词：

brand	size	look	cloth
for	try	pair	clothes

1. I need a new _____ of pants.

2. Jane is wearing new _____.

3. Do you have a piece of wet _____?

4. Can I have a _____ at your new car?
5. I wear _____ ten shoes.
6. May I _____ on these shoes?
7. What _____ of milk do you drink?
8. My father's old house is _____ sale.

II. Complete the dialogue: 完成下列会话 :

A: Can I t_____ a look at that shirt, please?
B: Sure. Here you are. It's on s_____.
A: Really? May I t_____ it on?
B: Sorry. You can't. What s_____ do you wear?
A: Medium. How m_____ is it?
B: It's only one hundred dollars.
A: OK. I'll t_____ it.
B: Good. H_____ you are.

Lesson 15

At the Department Store

在百货商店

1 *Dialogue* 会话

会话 A

A: Can you help me, please?

B: Sure. What can I do for you?

A: I'm looking for a gift for my son's birthday.

B: How about this video game?

A: That's a good idea. Can you gift-wrap it, please?

B: Sure. No problem.

A: 能不能请你帮我一个忙呢？

B: 当然。我能为您做什么？

A: 我正在为我儿子物色一个生日礼物。

B: 这个电子游戏如何？

A: 那倒是个好主意。可以请你把它用礼品纸包装起来吗？

B: 当然，没问题。

会话 B

A: Excuse me, ma'am. Do you have a blue dress my size?

B: I think so. Let me take your measurements. OK. How about this dress over here?

A: Do you have a fitting room?

B: It's in the corner over there.

A: Thank you.

B: You're welcome.

A: 女士，打扰一下。你这儿有合乎我尺寸的蓝色连衣裙吗？

B: 我想有的。让我量一下你的尺寸。好了，这边的这件连衣裙如何？

A: 你们有试衣间吗？

B: 就在那边的角落里。

A: 谢谢。

B: 不客气。

2 Vocabulary & Idioms 单词短语注解

会话 A

1. **department store** 百货商店
   department [dɪˈpɑrtmənt] 名 (公司、政府等的) 部门

2. **gift** [gɪft] 名 礼物

3. **son** [sʌn] 名 儿子
   daughter [ˈdɔtɚ] 名 女儿

4. **video game** [ˈvɪdɪoˌgem] 名 电子游戏，电玩
   video [ˈvɪdɪo] 形 电视的
   game [gem] 名 游戏

5. **idea** [aɪˈdiə] 名 主意；想法

6. **gift-wrap** [ˈgɪftˌræp] 动 (用包装纸、缎带等把物品) 包装 (成礼物)
   wrap [ræp] 动 包；裹
   Please wrap the baby in a blanket. 请把小宝宝包在毯子里。
   * blanket [ˈblæŋkɪt] 名 毛毯

会话 B

1. **blue** [blu] 形 蓝色的

2. **dress** [drɛs] 名 连衣裙，套裙

3. **think** [θɪŋk] 动 认为；想

4. **so** [so] 代 如此

5. **let** [lɛt] 动 让

6. **measurement** [ˈmɛʒɚmənt] 名 测量；尺寸，大小

7. **over here** 在这里，在这边
   over there 在那里，在那边

8. **fitting room** 试衣间

fitting [ˈfɪtɪŋ] 名 试衣, 试穿

9. **corner** [ˈkɔrnɚ] 名 角落

3 **_Grammar Points_ 语法重点** ∿

会话 A

1. **Can you help me, please?** 能不能请你帮我一个忙呢？

   = Can you do me a favor, please?

   = Can you give me a hand, please?

   a.　help＋人　帮某人忙, 帮助某人

   　=　do＋人＋a favor

   　=　give＋人＋a hand

   　　* favor [ˈfevɚ] 名 恩惠

   例 Will you do me a favor? 你愿意帮我一个忙吗？

   I need to move this table over there. Can you give me a hand?

   我必须把这张桌子移到那边去。你能帮我一下吗？

   b.　注意下列 "give＋人＋a hand" 与 "give＋人＋a big hand" 的区别：
   "give＋人＋a hand" 表示 "帮助某人" 的意思, 而 "give＋人＋a big hand" 则表示 "给某人热烈鼓掌" 之意。

   give＋人＋a hand　帮助某人

   give＋人＋a big hand　给某人热烈鼓掌

   例 A: Let me give you a hand with the box.

   　　B: Thanks a lot.

   　　A: 让我帮你拿那个箱子。

   　　B: 多谢。

   　　Let's give the speaker a big hand!

   　　咱们为这位演讲者热烈鼓掌！

2. **I'm looking for a gift for my son's birthday.**

   我正在为我儿子物色一样生日礼物。

   表示 "买/送东西给某人做为生日礼物" 有下列说法：

   例 I'm going to buy a necklace for my wife's birthday.

　　我要买一条项链给我太太作为生日礼物。

　= I'm going to buy a necklace <u>as</u> my wife's <u>birthday gift</u>.

　　I'll give my friend a book <u>for</u> her <u>birthday</u>.

　= I'll give my friend a book <u>as</u> her <u>birthday gift</u>.

　　我会送一本书给我朋友作为生日礼物。

3. **That's a good idea.** 那是个好主意。

在回应别人的提议、想法时，除了 "That's a good idea." 外，尚有下列类似用法：

That sounds like a good idea. 那听起来像是个好主意。

因为口语中经常使用，因此常将主语 That 省略，而简化为：

Sounds like a good idea. 听起来像是个好主意。

* sound [saʊnd] 动 听起来

* like [laɪk] 介 像……的

　例 A: Let's take a walk in the park. 咱们到公园里散个步吧。

　　　B: That's a good idea. 那是个好主意。

　　　= That sounds like a good idea. 那听起来像是个好主意。

　　　= Sounds like a good idea. 听起来像是个好主意。

会话 B

1. **Excuse me, <u>ma'am</u>. Do you have a blue dress <u>my size</u>?**

小姐，打扰一下。你们有合乎我尺寸的蓝色连衣裙吗？

　a. ma'am 是对女士的尊称，为 madam [ˈmædəm] 的简写。对男士的尊称则通常用 sir 一词。

　　例 Excuse me, ma'am. can you tell me the way to the train station?

　　　小姐，打扰一下。你可以告诉我到火车站的路怎么走吗？

　　　Good evening, sir. May I help you?

　　　晚上好，先生。我可以为你效劳吗？

　b. 上列句中的 my size 之前省略了介词 in，但实际使用时，in 不写出来。in my size 的字面意思为"在我的尺寸里面"，实际翻译则为"合乎我的尺寸"。

　　例 We have a shirt your size. 我们有一件合乎你尺寸的衬衫。

I'm sorry. We don't have any shoes your size.

很抱歉。我们没有合乎你尺寸的鞋子。

2. **I think so.** 我想有的。

上列句中的 so 是用来代替前面句中所提过的概念，表示"我认为如此。"、"我也这么想。"之意。

因此本句的 "I think so." 即下列句子的简化：

I think (that) we have a blue dress (in) your size.

例 A: Is this umbrella yours? 这把伞是你的吗？

B: I think so. 我想是的。

= I think this umbrella is mine.

若要表不同意对方的说法、想法或对某事不以为然时，则可说"I don't think so."表示。

例 A: Are we going to be late? 我们要迟到了吗？

B: I don't think so. 我不这么认为。

= I don't think we're going to be late.

3. **Let me take your measurements.** 让我量一下你的尺寸。

measurement 是指所量得的长度、高度、大小等；此处 "take your measurements" 中的 measurements 用复数，这是因为量身材时所量的部位不只一处（如腰围、肩宽、臂长等），因此要用复数。

例 What's your waist measurement? 你的腰围多粗？

* waist [west] 名 腰（部）

If you want to have a tailor-made suit, the tailor must take your measurements.

如果你想要订做西装，裁缝必须量你的尺寸。

* tailor-made [ˈteləˌmed] 形 订做的，定制的

* tailor [ˈtelə] 名 裁缝

4. **How about this dress over here?** 在这里的这件连衣裙如何？

a. here 与 there 均为副词，分别表示"（在）这里"、"（在）那里"，使用时通常置于句尾。

例 John is standing here. 约翰正站在这里。

I see a man there. 我看到那里有个人。

b. 在口语中，常常在 here 与 there 之前加 over 以加强其语气，表示"就在这里"、"就在那里"的距离感，不过翻译时，并不一定要翻成"就在这／那里"，可视情况而定。

例 The book you are looking for is over here. 你要找的书在这里。

Jack is next to the door over there. 杰克就在那里的门边。

5. **It's in the corner over there.** 就在那边的角落里。

in the corner 在角落里

on the corner 在转角处

around the corner 在转角附近

注意

in the corner 指的是在空间内的角落，on the corner 是指空间外的转角处，around the corner 则指转角附近。

例 Helen is sitting in the corner of the room. 海伦正坐在房间的角落里。

There's a grocery store on the corner. 在转角处有家杂货店。

Mary lives around the corner. 玛丽住在转角附近。

---

4   *Substitution* 替换   🎧

1. Can you 〔help me, / do me a favor, / give me a hand,〕 please? 能不能请你帮我一个忙呢？

2. That's / That sounds like / Sounds like 〕 a good idea.   那是个好主意。／那听起来像是个好主意。／听起来像是个好主意。

3. Do you have a blue dress 〔my size? / her size?〕

你们有合乎我／她尺寸的蓝色连衣裙吗？

4. How about the dress over 〔here? / there?〕

在这／那里的那件蓝色连衣裙如何？

5. It's | in / on / around | the corner over there.　就在那边的角落里。
就在那边的转角处。
就在那边的转角附近。

5 ***Exercises*** 练习 ☪

I. Use the right word: 请选出适当的单词 :

as	sounds	madam	corner
in	measurements	hand	favor

1. Can you give me a _____ with this heavy bag?
2. Can you do me a _____, please?
3. I want to buy a pen _____ my friend's birthday gift.
4. Your plan _____ like a good idea.
5. Excuse me, _____. Would you like to have a seat?
6. Do you have this shirt _____ size six?
7. There's a bank just around the _____.
8. Please stand up. I need to take your _____.

II. Complete the dialogue: 完成下列会话 :

A: Excuse me. Can I h____ you?

B: Yes. I'm l____ for a white shirt.

A: What s____ do you wear?

B: I'm not sure. Maybe large.

A: I don't think s____.

B: Maybe you should t____ my measurements.

A: That's a good i____. Let's go o____ there.

Lesson 16

At the Shoe Store

在鞋店

会话 A

A: Do you have these shoes in size 8?

B: Sure. Here you are.

A: I'm sorry, but they are too small. Do you have a
　 bigger pair?

B: Here. Try these on.

A: Wow! These are just right.

A: 你们这双鞋有没有 8 号的？

B: 当然。给您。

A: 对不起，这双太小了。你们有大一点的号吗？

B: 这儿。试穿看看。

A: 哇！这一双刚好。

会话 B

A: Excuse me. Can you show me some high-heeled shoes?

B: Sure. This way, please.

A: These are too high. Do you have lower ones?

B: How about these?

A: They don't fit. Do you have smaller ones?

B: I'm afraid we don't have your size.

A: What a shame!

A: 打扰一下。你能不能拿一些高跟鞋给我看？

B: 当然。请这边走。

A: 这些跟太高了。你们有低一点的吗？

B: 那这些如何？

A: 这些不合脚。你们有小一点的吗？

B: 恐怕我们没有你的尺寸。

A: 真可惜！

2 *Vocabulary & Idioms* 单词短语注解 ✍

会话 A

1. **shoe** [ʃu] 名 鞋

2. **small** [smɔl] 形 小的

3. **bigger** [ˈbɪgɚ] 形 较大的（是 big 的比较级）
   big [bɪg] 形 大的

4. **pair** [pɛr] 名 一双，一对，一副

5. **wow** [waʊ] 叹 哇！（表示惊奇、羡慕等）

6. **just** [dʒʌst] 副 正好，恰好

7. **right** [raɪt] 形 适当的，恰好的

会话 B

1. **show** [ʃo] 动 指出，指给……看

2. **high-heeled** [ˈhaɪˌhild] 形 高跟的
   high-heeled shoes 高跟鞋
   high [haɪ] 形 高的
   heeled [hild] 形 有后跟的
   heel [hil] 名 脚后跟；（鞋、袜等的）后跟
   注意
   high-heeled shoes 亦可用 high-heels [ˈhaɪˌhilz] 来表示。

3. **lower** [ˈloɚ] 形 较低／矮的（是 low 的比较级）
   low [lo] 形 低的；矮的

4. **one** [wʌn] 代 用以代替单数的事物或人（ones 为复数）

5. **fit** [fɪt] 动 适合，合身

6. **smaller** [ˈsmɔlɚ] 形 较小的（是 small 的比较级）

7. **I'm afraid...** 恐怕……
   afraid [əˈfred] 形 恐怕……的；害怕的

③ *Grammar Points* 语法重点

会话 A

1. **Do you have these shoes in size 8?**

   你们这双鞋有没有 8 号的？

   Do you have + 名词 + in size + 尺寸？

   你们有没有……（尺寸）的……（东西）呢？

   例 Customer: Do you have these socks in size nine?

   Clerk: Sure. This way, please.

   顾客：你们这双袜子有没有 9 号的？

   店员：当然有。请这边走。

   * customer [ˈkʌstəmɚ] 名 顾客
   * clerk [klɝk] 名 店员；职员

2. **Do you have a bigger pair?** 你们有大一点的号吗？

   pair 代表"一双、一对"，凡是成双或成对的物品，通常都要用 pair 这个词。例如：

   a pair of trousers / pants 一条裤子

   a pair of jeans 一条牛仔裤

   * jeans [dʒinz] 名 牛仔裤

   a pair of shorts 一条短裤

   * shorts [ʃɔrts] 名 短裤

   * 因裤子有两条裤管，故要用复数，因此无 a trouser / pant / short 之用法。如果说 a trouser / pant /short，那么穿的时候变成两只脚套在同一只裤管里，那肯定是会跌倒的。

   a pair of glasses 一副眼镜

   因为眼睛有两个，故有两个镜片，因此要用复数。

   a pair of scissors 一把剪刀

   scissors [ˈsɪzɚz] 名 剪刀

   * 因为剪刀要两个刀片才能剪，故要用复数。

3. **Wow! These are just right.** 哇！这一双刚好。

   wow 是感叹词，乃表示惊奇、羡慕等时所发出的声音；除了 wow 之外，还可以用 gee [dʒi] 或 gee-whiz [ˋdʒi,wɪz] 代替，不过 wow 通常用在好的方面，而 gee 或 gee-whiz 则好、坏方面都可使用。

例 A: My dad will buy me a new bike.

B: Wow! You're lucky.

A: 我爸爸要买一辆新的自行车给我。

B: 哇! 你真幸福。

A: My feet hurt. 我的脚好痛。

B: Gee! That's too bad. 哇! 太糟了。

会话 B

1. **Can you show me some high-heeled shoes?**

= Can you show me some high-heels?

你能不能拿一些高跟鞋给我看?

show + 人 + 东西　拿 / 将某物给某人看

例 Can you show me those earrings? 你能不能拿那些耳环给我看?

I'll show you my new watch tomorrow. 明天我会拿我的新表给你看。

在上述用法中，"人"之后亦可接"地方"形成下列用法:

show + 人 + 地方　指示某人往某地的路

例 Please show me the way to the train station.

请告诉我到火车站的路怎么走。

2. **These are too high. Do you have lower ones?**

这些跟太高了。你们有低一点的吗?

上列第二个句子中的 ones 是代词，用来代替前面已提过的名词 shoes。原句实为:

These (= These high-heeled shoes) are too high. Do you have lower high-heeled shoes?

但 high-heeled shoes 重复了一次，就修辞而言应予避免，故用 ones 代替。这个 ones 专用来代替前面已提过的复数名词，而 one 则是用来代替前面已提过的单数名词。

例 Those mangos are delicious, especially the red mangos. (劣)

→ Those mangos are delicious, especially the red ones. (佳)

那些芒果很好吃,尤其是红色的那些。

Jack wants <u>a new bike</u>, but he doesn't have enough money to buy <u>a new bike</u>. (劣)

→ Jack wants <u>a new bike</u>, but he doesn't have enough money to buy <u>one</u>. (佳)
杰克想要一辆新的自行车,但他没有足够的钱买。

3. **They don't fit.** 这些不合脚。

= They don't fit me.

fit 是动词,表"适合"、"合身"的意思,可以单独使用,也可以在后面加"人"作宾语。

例 Do these socks fit? 这双袜子合不合脚?

This jacket fits you very well. 这件夹克你穿起来很合身。

4. **I'm afraid we don't have your size.** 恐怕我们没有你的尺寸。

= I'm afraid <u>that</u> we don't have your size.

I'm afraid +(that) + 主语 + 动词 ... 恐怕……

注意

上述句型中,that 可以省略,直接在 I'm afraid 后面接另一个从句。这是一种要给人不愉快的讯息或消息时所用的婉转措词,表示"恐怕……"的意思。

例 I'm afraid (that) I have some bad news for you.
恐怕我有不好的消息要给你。

I'm afraid (that) we don't have what you want. 恐怕我们没有你要的。

④ Substitution 替换

1. Do you have | these shoes in size 8? 你们这些鞋有没有 8 号的?
              | this shirt in size 9? 你们这件衬衫有没有 9 号的?

2. Sure. | Here you are. | （较口语） 当然,给您。
   Of course. | | （较正式）

3. Do you have a | bigger | pair?
                 | smaller |
   你们有号码大一点 / 小一点的吗?

4. Can you show me some | high-heeled shoes?
                          | sunglasses?

你能不能拿一些高跟鞋 / 太阳眼镜给我看?

5. They | don't fit.
         | don't fit me.   这些不合我的尺寸。
         | aren't my size.

6. I'm afraid | we don't have your size. 恐怕我们没有你的尺寸。
               | I can't help you. 恐怕我无法帮你。

5 **Exercises** 练习 ☪

I. Use the right word: 请选出适当的单词:

that	pair	fit	Wow
one	size	ones	shame

1. We don't have these shoes in _____ ten.

2. I want to buy a _____ of dark glasses.

3. _____! What a pretty girl she is!

4. Gee! What a _____ you can't come!

5. These are nice shoes, but I'll buy the cheaper _____.

6. These shoes are too small. They don't _____.

7. I'm afraid _____ I don't have enough money.

8. I have two apples. Which _____ do you want?

II. Complete the dialogue: 完成下列会话:

A: Do you have jeans that will f_____ me?

B: What s_____ do you wear?

A: I don't know. Can I t_____ these on?

B: They are too small.

A: H_____ about these?

B: I'm a_____ they are too big.

A: Which o_____ should I try on?

B: This w_____, please.

Lesson 17

At the Bookstore
在书店

1   *Dialogue* 会话

会话 A

A: Excuse me. Do you have *A Tale of Two Cities*?

B: Who is the author?

A: Charles Dickens.

B: Sorry. We're sold out right now. Please come back next week.

A: OK. Thanks!

A: 打扰一下。你们有《双城记》这本书吗？

B: 作者是谁？

A: 查尔斯·狄更斯。

B: 很抱歉，我们现在卖完了。请下个星期再来。

A: 好的。多谢！

会话 B

A: Do you have a good English-Chinese dictionary?

B: Sure. How about this one?

A: Is this the latest edition?

B: Yes. We have both the paperback and the hardcover.

A: What's the difference?

B: The hardcover is more expensive.

A: Oh! I see. I'll have the paperback, please.

A: 你们有没有好的英汉词典?

B: 当然有。这一本如何?

A: 这是最新版本吗?

B: 是的。我们有平装本和精装本。

A: 有什么差别呢?

B: 精装本比较贵。

A: 噢! 我明白了。请给我平装本的。

2 Vocabulary & Idioms 单词短语注解

会话 A

1. **bookstore** [ˈbʊkˌstɔr] 名书店

2. **A Tale of Two Cities** 《双城记》(书名)
   tale [tel] 名故事
   city [ˈsɪtɪ] 名城市 (cities 是复数形式)

3. **author** [ˈɔθɚ] 名作者, 作家

4. **Charles Dickens** [ˈtʃɑrlz ˈdɪkɪnz] 名查尔斯·狄更斯 (1812-1870, 英国名小说家)

5. **be sold out** 全部卖 / 售完
   sold [sold] 是动词 sell 的过去分词。
   sell [sɛl] 动(贩)卖, (销)售
   I want to sell my old car. 我想卖掉我的旧车。

6. **next week** 下星期, 下周
   next [nɛkst] 形下一个的
   week [wik] 名一星期, 一周

7. **come back** 回来
   come [kʌm] 动来(到)
   Please come back an hour later. 请一个小时后再来。

会话 B

1. **English-Chinese** [ˈɪŋglɪʃˌtʃaɪˈniz] 形英汉的
   English [ˈɪŋglɪʃ] 形英语的 & 名英语
   Chinese [tʃaɪˈniz] 形中文的 & 名中文

2. **dictionary** [ˈdɪkʃənˌɛrɪ] 名词典

3. **latest** [ˈletɪst] 形最新的 ; 最近的 (是 late 的最高级)
   late [let] 形迟的, 晚的

4. **edition** [ɪˈdɪʃən] 名版, 版本

This is the fifth edition of this book. 这是这本书的第五版。

5. **both...and...** 既……且……，……以及……
   both [boθ] 连 两者都

6. **paperback** [ˈpepɚ͵bæk] 名 平装本 / 书

7. **hardcover** [ˈhɑrd͵kʌvɚ] 名 精装本 / 书

8. **difference** [ˈdɪfərəns] 名 不同，差异

3 *Grammar Points* 语法重点 〰

会话 A

1. **Do you have *A Tale of Two Cities*?** 你们有《双城记》这本书吗?
   a. tale 为"故事"的意思，是比较文诌诌的用法，一般口语中都用 story [ˈstɔrɪ] 一词表示。
      例 John likes to listen to stories. 约翰喜欢听故事。
   b. A Tale of Two cities 是书名，一般在印刷或打字时，要用斜体来表示；如果书写时，则在该书名下面划底线。
      例 *Pride and Prejudice* is my favorite novel.（印刷或打字）
      《傲慢与偏见》是我最喜欢的小说。
      Do you know the author of Pride and Prejudice?（书写）
      你知道《傲慢与偏见》的作者是谁吗?

2. **Sorry. We're sold out right now.** 很抱歉，我们现在卖完了。
   = I'm sorry. We're sold out right now.
   = I'm sorry, but we're sold out right now.
      上列中的"Sorry."是"I'm sorry."的简化；在口语中，经常可以使用"Sorry."一个词来代替"I'm sorry."。
      例 I'm sorry, but I can't go to your party tonight.
      = I'm sorry. I can't go to your party tonight.
      = Sorry. I can't go to your party tonight.
      很抱歉，今晚我无法去参加你的派对。

3. **We're sold out right now.** 我们现在卖完了。

"we're sold out"是常见的用法,意思是"我们卖完了",其中的 sold out 视作形容词,表示"卖完/光"的。

例 A: Do you have this book here? 你们这儿有这本书吗?

　　B: I'm sorry, but we're sold out. 很抱歉,我们已经卖完了。

注意

表示"我们已经将某东西卖完了"有下列两种用法:

a.　we're sold out of + 东西

　　例 We're sold out of shoes in your size.

　　　你那尺寸的鞋子我们已全卖完了。

b.　we have sold out of + 东西

　　例 We have sold out of milk. 我们的牛奶已经全卖完了。

　　注意

　　上述用法是"sell out of..."的现在完成时,也就是"have + sold out of + 宾语",其中的 have 称为现在完成时助动词,译成"已经";此种现在完成时的句型如下:

　　主语 + have / has + 过去分词　……已经……

　　译 他将会离开。

　　　He will leave.

　　译 他已经离开了。

　　　He has left.(left [lɛft] 是 leave [liv] 的过去分词)

　　译 他们将会去美国。

　　　They will go to the States.

　　译 他们已经去美国了。

　　　They have gone to the States.(gone [gɔn] 是 go 的过去分词)

4.　**Please come back next week.** 请下个星期再来。

　　next week 是"下个星期"的意思;同理,表示"下(一)个……(时间)"我们通常都可用"next + 时间名词"来表示。例如:

　　next month 下个月

　　next year 明年

　　next Sunday 下个星期日

　　next Saturday 下个星期六

例 John will graduate from college next month.

约翰下个月将从大学毕业。

* graduate [ˈɡrædʒʊˌet] 动 毕业
* college [ˈkɑlɪdʒ] 名 大学

They will get married next year. 他们明年要结婚了。

* get married 结婚
* marry [ˈmærɪ] 动 结婚

I'll see you next Monday. 下个星期一见。

会话 B

1. **Do you have a good English-Chinese dictionary?**

   你们有没有好的英汉词典?

   "English-Chinese dictionary"指的是"英汉词典","汉英词典"的说法为"Chinese-English dictionary","英英词典"的说法则为"English-English dictionary";读者要知道的是,我们在念这种中间有连字符(即"-")的词时,只要把两旁的单词念出来就可以了,而不用把连词号的英文"hyphen"[ˈhaɪfən] 也说出来。例如 English-Chinese 的念法为 [ˈɪŋɡlɪʃˌtʃaɪˈniz],而不是 [ˈɪŋɡlɪʃ, ˈhaɪfən, ˌtʃaɪˈniz]。

   注意

   我们在学英文时,一定时常会碰到单词或不懂的用法,这个时候我们就要去查词典,这"查词典"的英文就可以说"consult the dictionary";如果是"在词典里查单词",这时就要用"look up the word in the dictionary"。也就是说,"查词典"的动词要用 consult,"查单词"的动词要用 look up,可不要说成"look up the dictionary"。

   * consult [kənˈsʌlt] 动 查阅

   例 I will consult the dictionary for the meaning of that word.

   我会在词典里查那个单词的意思。

   I must look up that difficult word in the dictionary.

   我必须在词典里查那个难理解的单词。

2. **Is this the latest edition?** 这是最新版本吗?

The hardcover is more expensive. 精装本比较贵。

以上的第一句中的 latest 为形容词 late 的最高级，与定冠词 the 连用；第二句中的 more expensive 则为形容词 expensive 的比较级。我们在 Lesson 12 已提过形容词的比较级变化，在本课中我们将再做一些复习及补充说明，并介绍形容词的最高级变化，兹说明如下：

不管是在中文或英文中均有原级、比较级和最高级的用语，例如：

中文：她很漂亮。（"漂亮"是原级）

英文：She is beautiful.（beautiful 是原级）

中文：我比她更漂亮

　　　＊"更漂亮"是"漂亮"的比较级。

英文：I am more beautiful than she.

　　　＊ more beautiful 是 beautiful 的比较级；more 是"更"的意思，than 则译成"比"。

中文：她是我们班上最漂亮的女孩。

　　　＊"最漂亮"是"漂亮"的最高级。

英文：She is the most beautiful girl in our class.

　　　＊ most beautiful 是 beautiful 的最高级，要与定冠词 the 连用。

一般而言，形容词的比较级和最高级变化有下列原则：

a. 原则是双音节或三音节以上的形容词：

　　比较级：more ＋原级

　　最高级：most ＋原级

原级	比较级	最高级
expensive [ɪkˈspɛnsɪv] 昂贵的	more expensive 较贵的	most expensive 最贵的
beautiful [ˈbjutəfəl] 漂亮的	more beautiful 较漂亮的	most beautiful 最漂亮的

b. 原级是单音节的形容词：

　　比较级：原级 ＋ -er

　　最高级：原级 ＋ -est

原级	比较级	最高级
small [smɔl] 小的	smaller 较小的	smallest 最小的
low [lo] 低的 / 矮的	lower 较低 / 矮的	lowest 最低 / 矮的

c.　原级是以辅音结尾的单音节形容词：

比较级：重复该辅音字母 + -er

最高级：重复该辅音字母 + -est

原级	比较级	最高级
hot [hɑt] 炎热的	hotter 较热的	hottest 最热的
fat [fæt] 肥胖的	fatter 较胖的	fattest 最胖的

d.　原级是以 -e 结尾的单音节形容词，或以 -le 结尾的双音节形容词：

比较级：原级 + -r

最高级：原级 + -st

原级	比较级	最高级
wise [waɪz] 有智慧的	wiser 较有智慧的	wisest 最有智慧的
gentle [ˈdʒɛntl̩] 温和的	gentler 较温和的	gentlest 最温和的

e.　形容词结尾为"辅音 + -y"时：

比较级：将 y 改成 i + -er

最高级：将 y 改成 i + -est

原级	比较级	最高级
pretty [ˋprɪtɪ] 美丽的	prettier 较美丽的	prettiest 最美丽的
easy [ˋizɪ] 容易的	easier 较容易的	easiest 最容易的

f. 以上的比较级和最高级变化称作规则变化。但也有些形容词则呈不规则变化。如：

原级	比较级	最高级
good [gʊd] 好的	better [ˋbɛtɚ] 较好的	best [bɛst] 最好的
bad [bæd] 坏的	worse [wɝs] 较坏的	worst [wɝst] 最坏的

所幸这些不规则变化的形容词并不多，只要读者多阅读英文文章，见到一个就记一个，自然就会熟悉这些不规则变化的形容词。

g. 关于形容词的最高级尚有一点要注意的是：
形容词的最高级要与定冠词 the 连用。

例 John is a best student in his class. (✕)
John is the best student in his class. (✓)
约翰是他班上最好的学生。

3. **We have both the paperback and the hardcover.**
= We have both the paperback dictionaries and the hardcover dictionaries.
我们有平装本和精装本。

a. 上列句中在 paperback 和 hardcover 之后省略了 dictionaries 一词，因语意已非常清楚。故不须再重复此词。

b. "both...and..." 表示 "……和 / 以及……" 的意思，及 "...and..." 的强调用法，而且只限于表示两者时使用。

例 Both Peter and Carlos are very smart.
彼得和卡洛斯两人都很聪明。

4. **What's the difference?** 平装本和精装本之间有什么差别呢？

= What's the difference between the paperback and the hardcover?

the difference between A and B　A 与 B 之间的差异 / 不同

例 The difference between Jack and Jeff is not big.

杰克和杰夫之间的差异并不大。

④ *Substitution* 替换　　　　　♋

1. Who is the ⎰author?　作者是谁？
　　　　　　　⎱writer?

　* writer [ˈraɪtɚ] 名 作者，作家

2. Please come back next ⎰week.
　　　　　　　　　　　⎱Friday.
　　　　　　　　　　　⎱month.

请下个星期 / 下个星期五 / 下个月再来。

3. Do you have a good ⎰English-Chinese⎱
　　　　　　　　　　⎱Chinese-English⎱ dictionary?
　　　　　　　　　　⎱English-English⎱

你们有没有好的英汉 / 汉英 / 英英词典？

4. We have both the paperback and the hardcover.
I like both jazz and rock 'n' roll.
Both he and I are students.

我们有平装本和精装本。

我喜欢爵士乐以及摇滚乐。

他和我都是学生。

　* rock 'n' roll　摇滚乐
　= rock and roll

5. The hardcover is more expensive. 精装本比较贵。
Lily is more beautiful than Helen. 莉莉比海伦更漂亮。
David is taller than Tom. 大卫比汤姆高。

5 *Exercises* 练习

I. Use the right word: 请选出适当的单词 :

| next | smaller | of | but |
| more | look | consult | gone |

1. I'm sorry. We're sold out _____ blue pens.
2. I'm sorry, _____ John's not here.
3. Mr. Li has _____ to the States.
4. Miss Wang will get married _____ week.
5. Please _____ the dictionary for the meaning of this word.
6. Linda is _____ beautiful than her sister.
7. This desk is _____ than mine.
8. I'll _____ up the word in the dictionary.

II. Complete the dialogue: 完成下列会话 :

A: I need a good Chinese-English d_____ .

B: Is this o_____ OK?

A: Is this t_____ best one you have?

B: No. But it is the cheapest.

A: Do you have a b_____ one?

B: Yes. But it is more e_____ .

A: Oh，I see. Is this the l_____ edition?

B: Yes.

A: OK. I'll t_____ it.

Lesson 18

Taking a Taxi
搭乘出租车

1 *Dialogue* 会话

A: Where to, ma'am?

B: The train station, please.

A: (arrives) Here we are, ma'am.

B: How much do I owe you?

A: It's 135 Yuan on the meter.

B: Here's 150 Yuan. Keep the change.

A: Thanks!

A: 小姐，你要到哪里去？

B: 麻烦到火车站。

A: （抵达后）小姐，到了。

B: 要给你多少钱？

A: 里程表上是 135 元。

B: 这里是 150 元钱。零钱不用找了。

A: 多谢！

会话 B

A: To the airport, please.

B: The international or domestic one?

A: The international airport.

B: Got it!

A: Could you speed up, please? I don't want to miss my flight.

B: What time's your flight?

A: 10:45 p.m.

B: Don't worry! I'll get you there in time.

A: 麻烦到机场。

B: 国际机场还是国内机场？

A: 国际机场。

B: 知道了。

A: 麻烦能请你开快一点吗？ 我不想误了我的班机。

B: 您的班机是几点？

A: 晚上 10 点 45 分。

B: 别担心！ 我会及时把您送到那儿去。

2 *Vocabulary & Idioms* 单词短语注解 ✎

会话 A

1. **take a taxi** 搭乘出租车
   take [tek] 动 搭乘（交通工具）
   taxi [ˈtæksɪ] 名 出租车

2. **train station** 火车站
   train [tren] 名 火车

3. **arrive** [əˈraɪv] 动 抵达，到达

4. **Here we are.** （我们）到了（目的地）。

5. **owe** [o] 动 欠（债）

6. **meter** [ˈmitɚ] 名 里程表；计量器

7. **keep the change** （零钱）不用找了
   keep [kip] 动 保留，保持，保存

会话 B

1. **airport** [ˈɛrˌport] 名 机场

2. **international** [ˌɪntɚˈnæʃənḷ] 形 国际的

3. **domestic** [dəˈmɛstɪk] 形 国内的，本国的

4. **Got it!** 了解 / 知道 / 明白了！
   = I've got it!

5. **speed up** 加快速度
   speed [spid] 动 加速，增速

6. **want** [wɑnt] 动 想要

7. **miss** [mɪs] 动 错过，未赶上

8. **flight** [flaɪt] 名 （飞机的）飞行航班，班机

9. **worry** [ˈwɝɪ] 动 担心，忧虑

10. **in time** 及时，来得及

3 *Grammar Points* 语法重点

标题

1. 我们一般要表示"搭乘"某种交通工具时，动词通常用 **take** 来表示，此时在该交通工具前要置不定冠词 **a / an** 或定冠词 **the**，如：

   take the / a taxi 乘出租车

   take the / a bus 乘公交车

   take the / a train 乘火车

   take the / an airplane 乘飞机

   take the / a ship / boat 乘船

   例 Let's take a taxi to the restaurant. 咱们乘出租车到那家餐厅去吧。

   Jimmy takes the bus to school every day. 吉米每天乘公交车上学。

   We must take a boat to get to that island.

   我们必须乘船才能到那座岛上。

2. 除了用动词 **take** 来表示"搭乘"某种交通工具外，也可用"介词 **by** + 交通工具"来表示。

   但此时该交通工具前不可置任何冠词（a, an, the），如：by taxi（乘出租车）、by bus（乘公交车）、by train（乘火车）、by ship / boat（乘船）、by airplane / plane（乘飞机）、by bicycle（骑自行车）等。

   因此上列第一句及第二句亦可写成：

   Let's go to the restaurant by taxi.

   Jimmy goes to school by bus every day.

   例 We will go to the States by plane tomorrow.

   我们明天要乘飞机去美国。

3. 若要表示"步行"时，则可以用 **"on foot"**。

   例 The only way to get to the village is on foot.

   到那个村庄去的唯一途径是步行。

会话 A

1. **Where to, ma'am?** 小姐，你要到哪里去？

   = Where are you going, ma'am?

这是一般乘客上了出租车后，司机询问乘客要到哪里去的问句；直接说 "Where to, ma'am / sir?"（小姐 / 先生，你要到哪里去？）是较简化的口语用法，但 Where to 实由 Where are you going? 简化而来，因为经常使用而变成了习惯语。

例 Taxi driver: Where to, sir?

Passenger : The Palace Museum, please.

出租车司机：先生，你要到哪里去？

乘客：麻烦到故宫博物院。

2. **Here we are, ma'am.** 小姐，我们到了。

以下是一些有关 here 及 there 起首的习惯用语，这些都是很常用的句子，希望读者能熟悉这些用法：

a. Here we are. （我们）到了。

解说

某甲要去见某女生，但胆小如鼠，于是便请某乙陪他一块去。两人乘了一部出租车，到了该女生家门口时，某甲、某乙以及出租车司机都可说这句话："Here we are."。

b. Here you are / go. 在这儿 / 拿去吧。

= There you go.

解说

某甲到麦当劳买汉堡，服务小姐叫他稍候片刻。不久，服务小姐就把汉堡递给某甲，同时说了一句："Here you go."；所以我们知道，给任何人所要的东西时，均可使用 "Here you are."、"Here you go." 及 "There you go."。

c. There you are. 在那里 / 原来你在这儿。

解说

（1）某甲要到朋友家去，由于是第一次拜访，在小区里找了老半天，仍然不得其门而入，幸好某乙刚好路过，见状即带路，到了某甲的朋友家后某乙即可说道："There you are." 或 "There it is."。

（2）除了上述情况外，我们到处找某人遍寻不着而最后终于找到时，也可以用 "There you are." 这句话。例如：某甲有急事找某乙，他把某乙可能去的地方都找遍了，仍不见他的人影，后来不小心在路上看到某乙，这时某甲就可以对某乙说：

There you are! Where have you been? I've been looking all over for you.

原来你在这儿！你跑到哪里去了？我一直到处在找你。

d. There you go again. 你又来（这一套）了 / 你老毛病又犯了。

解说

小强很不喜欢上学，所以经常编借口找理由不去学校；在一个寒流来袭的冬天早上，小强告诉妈妈说他牙齿痛无法去上课，由于这个理由小强上个礼拜已经用过了，于是妈妈就对小强说道："There you go again."（你又来了。），然后还是押着小强去上学。

3. **How much do I owe you?** 我要给你多少钱？

owe 是动词，表示"欠（债）"的意思，此处乘客问欠司机多少钱，也就是在问要给司机多少车钱的意思。有关 owe 的用法如下：

owe＋人＋金钱 欠某人……（金钱）

例 A: I remember you still owe me US$10. 我记得你还欠我 10 美元。

B: Really? 真的吗？

4. **Keep the change.** 零钱不用找了。

我们下出租车要给司机车费，或是去买东西给钱时，要把剩下找的零钱给对方当小费时，就可以用"Keep the change."。

例 Clerk: That'll be 90 Yuan, please.

Customer: Here's a hundred. Keep the change.

店员：麻烦总共要 90 元。

顾客：这儿是 100 元。不用找了。

会话 B

1. **To the airport, please.** 麻烦到机场。

= Take me to the airport, please.

表"（用车）载某人到某地"可用下列句型：

take + 人 + to + 地方

例 Helen takes her daughter to school every morning.

海伦每天早上都载她女儿去上学。

2. **The international or domestic one?**

= Do you want me to take you to the international airport or the domestic airport?

你要我载你到国际机场还是国内机场?

本句中的 one 用来代替前一句中的 airport; 我们在 Lesson 16 Part B 中, 已提过用 one 及 ones 代替前面已提过的单数名词和复数名词之用法, 这里仅再提供例句供读者参考。

例 Would you like this pen or the red one?

你想要这支笔还是红色的那支?

These apples are good, but I prefer the green ones there.

这些苹果都不错, 但是我比较喜欢青色的那些。

* prefer [prɪˈfɚ] 动 较喜欢

3. **Got it!** 知道了!

"Got it!" 是极口语的用法, 表示 "知道了!"、"我明白了!" 或 "我了解了!" 的意思, 也就等于 "I see." 或 "I understand."。

例 A: Just follow this map and you won't get lost. Got it?

B: Got it!

A: 只要照着这张地图走你就不会迷路, 知道吗?

B: 知道了!

4. **Could you speed up, please?** 麻烦能请你开快一点吗?

speed up 是 "加速" 的意思, 其反义词是 slow down(慢下来), 这两个短语也是常见的用法。

例 A: I'm in a hurry. Could you speed up, please?

B: No problem.

A: 我在赶时间。可以请你开快一点吗?

B: 没问题。

Slow down! You're driving too fast. 慢一点! 你开得太快了。

5. **I don't want to miss my flight.** 我不想错过我的班机。

a. 此处的 miss 是动词，表"错过，未赶上"的意思。

例 If you miss the bus, you'll be late.

你如果误了这班公交车就会迟到。

* if [ɪf] 连 如果，假设

b. miss 除了当"错过"外，还可以作"想念"的意思。

例 Jim misses his mom's cooking very much.

吉姆很想念他妈妈煮的菜。

6. **Don't worry!** 别担心！

例 A: Don't worry! Everything will be OK. 别担心！一切都会没事的。

B: I hope so. 我希望如此。

7. **I'll get you there in time.** 我会及时把你送到那儿去。

= I'll get you to the airport in time.

in time 及时

on time 准时

in time 表"及时"，是指在预定时间前一两分钟；而 on time 则是"准时"或"按时"，指刚刚好在预定时间。

in time 除可单独使用外，亦常常在后面加"for + 名词"或"to + 动词原形"，表"及时赶上（做）……"之意。

例 Am I in time for dinner? 我及时赶上吃晚餐吗？

You're just in time to help us paint the wall.

你刚好及时赶上帮我们油漆墙壁。

I'm sure we will finish the project on time.

我确信我们能准时搞完这个项目。

4 *Substitution* 替换

1. Let's take a | taxi / bus | to the restaurant.

= Let's go to the restaurant by | taxi. / bus.

咱们乘出租车 / 公交车到那家餐厅去吧。

2. We will go to the States by $\begin{vmatrix} \text{plane} \\ \text{ship} \end{vmatrix}$ tomorrow.

    我们明天要乘飞机 / 坐船去美国。

3. Where to,
    Where are you going, $\Big|$ ma'am? 小姐，你要到哪里去？

4. To the $\begin{vmatrix} \text{airport,} \\ \text{train station,} \end{vmatrix}$ please. 麻烦到机场 / 火车站。

5. Could you $\begin{vmatrix} \text{speed up,} \\ \text{slow down,} \end{vmatrix}$ please? 麻烦能请你开快 / 慢一点吗？

6. I don't want to miss $\begin{vmatrix} \text{my flight.} \\ \text{train.} \end{vmatrix}$ 我不想误了我的班机 / 火车。

5   *Exercises* 练习   ☪

I. Use the right word: 请选出适当的单词：

speed	in	keep	owes
take	one	by	foot

1. He goes to school _____ train every day.

2. I go to the office on _____ every morning.

3. It's faster if you _____ the plane.

4. He _____ most of his friends money.

5. Could you _____ up? You're driving too slowly.

6. If you don't have coins, just _____ the change.

7. I don't like this shirt. Can I have a look at that _____?

8. Come in! You're just _____ time for lunch.

II. Complete the dialogue: 完成下列会话：

A: How do you get to school, Jim?

B: I go on f_____. And you?

A: I t_____ the bus.

B: How come you go b_____ bus but don't get to school o_____ time
   sometimes?

A: The traffic is sometimes very bad.

B: Oh, I see. By the way, you'd better hurry, or you'll m____ your bus.

A: T_____ you go again, always worrying!

Lesson 19

Booking a Room
订房间

1 *Dialogue* 会话

会话 A

A: Excuse me. Do you have a single room?

B: Sorry. We're fully booked. The only room available at the moment is a twin room.

A: OK. I'll take it.

B: May I have your name, please?

A: I'm John Li.

B: How many days do you want to stay?

A: Five days.

A: 请问一下，你们有单人房吗？

B: 很抱歉，我们全订满了。目前唯一的空房是双人房。

A: 好，我就要双人房。

B: 请问尊姓大名？

A: 我是李约翰。

B: 您想要住几天呢？

A: 5 天。

会话 B

A: Excuse me. My name is Jack Wu. I'd like to book a room.

B: Single or double?

A: What are the rates?

B: It's US$100 for a single and US$150 for a double.

A: I'll take a single for 3 days.

B: OK. Just come to the front desk at the lobby.

A: OK. I'll arrive tomorrow.

B: See you then.

A: 麻烦你，我的名字是吴杰克，我想要订房间。

B: 您要单人房还是双人房？

A: 房价怎么算？

B: 单人房是 100 美元，而双人房是 150 美元。

A: 我要一间单人房，住 3 天。

B: 好。请到大厅的前台来就行了。

A: 好的。我明天到。

B: 到时候见。

2   *Vocabulary & Idioms* 单词短语注解

会话 A

1. **book** [bʊk] 动 预订（座位、房间等）

2. **single** [ˈsɪŋɡl] 形 单一的，单人用的
   single room 单人房

3. **fully** [ˈfʊlɪ] 副 完全地；充分地

4. **available** [əˈveləbl] 形 可用的，可获得的；有空的

5. **twin** [twɪn] 形 成对的；双胞胎的 & 名 双胞胎（之一）
   twin room（有两张单人床的）双人房
   The twins look exactly the same. 那对双胞胎看起来一模一样。

6. **How many + 复数名词?** 多少……?
   many [ˈmɛnɪ] 形 很多的，许多
   How many students are there in the classroom?
   教室里有多少个学生?

7. **stay** [ste] 动 留，停留，逗留
   I'll stay here for three days. 我会在这里待 3 天。

会话 B

1. **double** [ˈdʌbl] 形 双的，两倍的
   double room（有一张双人床或两张单人床的）双人房

2. **rate** [ret] 名 价格，费用

3. **lobby** [ˈlɑbɪ] 名（公共场所出入口处的）大厅

4. **arrive** [əˈraɪv] 动 到达，抵达
   Tommy usually arrives at school at 7:00 a.m.
   汤米通常在早上 7 点抵达学校。

5. **See you then.** 到时候见。
   then [ðɛn] 副（在）那时

3 **Grammar Points** 语法重点

标题

1. 我们要"预订"旅馆房间、飞机票、餐厅座位或门票等时， 都可以
   用 **book** 来表示。

   例 I am going to book a suite at the hotel in Tokyo.
   我要在东京的旅馆订一间套房。
   I will book two seats for tonight's concert.
   我会去订两个今晚音乐会的座位。

   * concert [ˈkɑnsət] 名 音乐会, 演唱会
     但 book 亦可作名词, 表示"书本"的意思。

   例 There are three books on the desk. 书桌上有 3 本书。

2. 表示"预订"、"预约"、"订票"等除了用 **book** 外， 还可以用
   reserve 或 **make a reservation** 来表示， 因此上列例句亦可写
   成：

   I am going to reserve a suite at the hotel in Tokyo.
   = I am going to make a reservation for a suite at the hotel in Tokyo.
   I will reserve two seats for tonight's concert.
   = I will make a reservation for two seats for tonight's concert.

   * reserve [rɪˈzɝv] 动 预订（旅馆、座位、门票等）
   * reservation [ˌrɛzəˈveʃən] 名（旅馆、座位、门票等的）预订, 不过在这
     三种用法中, 以 book 较为口语, 也最常用。

会话 A

1. **Do you have a single room?** 你们有单人房吗?
   旅馆或饭店的房间通常分为下列数种：
   single room（有一张单人床的）单人房
   twin room（有两张单人床的）双人房
   double room（有一张双人床或两张单人床的）双人房
   suite [swit]（备有卧房、客厅及浴室的）套房
   deluxe suite 豪华套房

* deluxe [dɪˈlʌks] 形 豪华的
  presidential suite 总统套房
* presidential [ˌprɛzəˈdɛnʃəl] 形 总统的

2. **Sorry. We're fully booked.** 很抱歉，我们全订满了。
   fully booked 是很常见的用法，表示旅馆房间、座位、餐桌、门票等
   已全被预订完了时，就可用 fully booked。其中 fully 是副词，表"完
   完全全地"，booked 作形容词，表"预订的"。

   例 A: I'd like to book a table for four tonight.
   　　B: Sorry. We're fully booked.
   　　A: 我想订今晚一张四个人坐的餐桌。
   　　B: 很抱歉，我们全订满了。

3. **The only room available at the moment is a twin room.**
   目前唯一的空房是双人房。
   一般的形容词修饰名词时，多置于该名词的前面。

   例 Mary is a pretty girl. 玛丽是个漂亮的女孩。
   　　John lives in a big house. 约翰住在一间大房子里。

   但在英文中，有少数形容词修饰名词时，形容词要放在该名词之
   后，而不可置于其前，如本句的 available 就是属于这类的形容词，
   因此我们不能说：

   The only available room at the moment is a twin room. (×)

   例 The only available doctor in the hospital does not have much
   　　experience. (×)
   → The only doctor available in the hospital does not have much
   　　experience. (√)
   　　这家医院唯一有空的一位医生没什么经验。

   * experience [ɪkˈspɪrɪəns] 名 经验

4. **How many days do you want to stay?** 您想要住几天呢？
   在中文里，虽然我们会说"住"旅馆，但在英文中却不用 live 这个
   词，而要用 stay（停留、待），因为使用 live 时，是指长期居住在某
   个地方，把那个地方当作家一样，而住在旅馆只是短期的行为，所
   以要用 stay 这个词。因此本问句不可说成：

How many days do you want to live? (×)

例 I have lived in Beijing for three years. 我已经在北京住了 3 年了。

I'll stay in that hotel when I am in New York.

我去纽约时会住在那家旅馆。

同理，如果你这个周末要待在朋友家里过夜时，也要用 stay，但如果你是和朋友住在一起的话，那就可以用 live。

例 This weekend I'm going to stay (over) at a friend's house.

这个周末我要待在朋友家过夜。

I live with a friend in a small apartment.

我和朋友住在一间小公寓里。

* apartment [ə`pɑrtmənt]名 公寓

会话 B

1. **Single or double?** 您想要订单人房还是双人房？

= Do you want to book a single or a double room?

2. **What are the rates?** 房价怎么算？

= What are the charges?

rate 及 charge [tʃɑrdʒ] 指 "价格"、"费用"，使用时一般都用复数 rates 及 charges，住旅馆或请人当家教时都可使用。

例 What are your rates for tutoring at a student's home?

你到学生家里去当家教的费用怎么算？

* tutor [`tjutɚ]动 当家庭教师 & 名 家庭教师

rate 除了表示 "价格"、"费用" 外，还可作 "速度 / 率" 的意思，有下列用法：

at the rate of... 以……的速度 / 率

例 The chicken lays eggs at the rate of one a day.

那只鸡一天下一个蛋。

* lay [le]动 下 / 生 (蛋)

3. **It's US$100 for a single and US$150 for a double.**

= It's US$100 for a single room and US$150 for a double room.

单人房是 100 美元，而双人房是 150 美元。

上列句中，US$100（100 美元）的念法为"one hundred US dollars"
而不是"US dollars one hundred"；同理，US$150 念成"one hundred
fifty US dollars"，而非"US dollars one hundred fifty"。

有关于表"金钱"的写法，除了把货币名称置于数字前面外，还可
以把数字写在前面，这时代表钱的符号"$"就不用写出来了，如：

US$100 = 100 US（dollars）

US$150 = 150 US（dollars）

4. **See you then.** 到时候见。

= See you at that time.

= See you when you arrive.

一般表示"再见"的说法有："Bye"、"Goodbye."、"See you."及"See
you later."；但如果有约定时间再见面时，这时我们就可以在"See
you."后面加上 then（到那时），形成"See you then."的用法，表示
"到时候见。"的意思。

例 A: Don't forget our date tomorrow night at 8 p.m.

B: I won't. See you then.

A: 别忘了我们明晚 8 点的约会。

B: 我不会忘的。到时候见了。

4 *Substitution* 替换 ◯ᴏ

1.	Do you have a	single room?	你们有单人房吗？
		twin room?	你们有两张单人床的双人房吗？
		double room?	你们有一张双人床或两张单人床的双人房吗？
		suite?	你们有套房吗？

| 2. | How many days / How long | do you want to stay? | 你要住几天呢？ / 你要住多久呢？ |

3.	I'd like to book	a room.	我想要订房间。
		two tickets to Taipei.	我想订两张到台北的票。
		a table for twelve.	我想订一张 12 个人坐的餐桌。

4. See you | then. | 到时候见。
    | at that time. |

5 *Exercises* 练习 ☪

I. Use the right word: 请选出适当的单词 :

See	rates	rate	then
stay	booked	make	lived

1. Tom has _____ a table for two at the new restaurant.

2. I'd like to _____ a reservation for a room.

3. May I _____ overnight at your home?

4. Tom has _____ in America for two years.

5. What are your _____ for teaching golf?

6. These books are selling at the _____ of 100 a week.

7. I have to go now. _____ you.

8. I'll arrive at about ten tonight. See you _____.

II. Complete the dialogue: 完成下列会话 :

A: Do you have any seats a _____ for tonight's concert?

B: Yes. But you must b _____ early.

A: I'd like to make a r _____ now.

B: Okay. Do you want to know the r _____ for the different types of tickets?

A: Just r _____ the cheapest kind for me.

B: Sure. How m _____ do you want?

A: Just two. How much are they?

B: They'll cost you 1,000 US d _____.

Lesson 20

Checking into a Hotel
办理住宿手续

1 *Dialogue* 会话

会话 A

A: Good morning. I'm Mr. Jack Wu. I have a reservation for a suite.

B: Oh, yes, Mr. Wu. Please fill out this form.

A: Here you are.

B: Will you pay by cash or charge?

A: Do you take traveler's checks?

B: Certainly.

A: 早上好。我是吴杰克。我预订了一间套房。

B: 哦，有的，吴先生。请填一下这张表格。

A: 拿去吧。

B: 您要付现金还是刷卡？

A: 你们收旅行支票吗？

B: 当然收。

会话 B

A: Excuse me. I'd like to check in, please. My name is Jack Wu.

B: One moment, please. Oh, yes. You have a reservation for a single room, right?

A: That's right.

B: May I have a look at your passport?

A: Here you go.

B: OK. You're booked in Room 609. Do you have any luggage?

A: Yes. These two suitcases.

B: No problem. The bellboy will take them and show you to your room.

A: 打扰一下，我想办理住宿手续。我是吴杰克。

B: 请稍等一下。哦，有的。您订了一间单人房，对不对？

A: 没错。

B: 我可以看一下您的护照吗？

A: 拿去吧。

B: 好了。您预订的是 609 号房。您有行李吗？

A: 有的。就这两个手提箱。

B: 没问题。服务生会拿行李并带您到房间去。

② *Vocabulary & Idioms* 单词短语注解

会话 A

1. **check into a hotel** 在旅馆办理住宿手续
   hotel [ho'tɛl] 名 旅馆，饭店

2. **reservation** [ˌrɛzɚ'veʃən] 名（旅馆房间、座位等的）预订

3. **suite** [swit] 名 套房

4. **fill out...** 填写……（文件、表格等）
   fill [fɪl] 动 填满；填补

5. **form** [fɔrm] 名 表格

6. **pay by cash** 用现金支付，付现金
   pay [pe] 动 付（钱）
   cash [kæʃ] 名 现金

7. **charge** [tʃɑrdʒ] 名 记账；收费

8. **traveler's check** 旅行支票
   traveler ['trævl̩ɚ] 名 旅行者，游客
   check [tʃɛk] 名 支票

9. **certainly** ['sɝtn̩lɪ] 副 当然，一定，的确

会话 B

1. **check in**（在旅馆）登记办理住宿手续
   check out（在旅馆）办理退房手续

2. **One moment, please.** 请稍候。

3. **passport** ['pæsˌpɔrt] 名 护照

4. **Here you go.** 在这儿／拿去吧。
   = Here you are.

5. **be booked in Room** ＋ 数字　预订……（号码）的房间
   I'm booked in Room 215. What about you?

我预订的房间是 215 号。你呢?

6. **luggage** [ˈlʌgɪdʒ] 名 行李(不可数名词)

7. **suitcase** [ˈsutˌkes] 名 手提箱

8. **bellboy** [ˈbɛlˌbɔɪ] 名(旅馆中帮人提行李或送东西等的)男服务生

9. **show** + 人 + **to** + 地方　将某人带到某地
   I'll show you to your table. 我会带你们到餐桌去。

③ *Grammar Points* 语法重点

标题

1. **"check into a / the hotel"** 是指在旅馆或饭店登记办理住宿的手续,也就等于 **check in (at a / the hotel)** 的用法。
   例 We will check into a hotel as soon as we get to Taichung.
   我们一抵达台中就会去饭店办理住宿手续。
   Let's check in before we have lunch at the hotel.
   咱们先在饭店办住宿手续再吃午餐吧。

2. 如果要表示"办理退房手续"时,则可以用 **check out (of a / the hotel)** 这个短语。
   例 The clerk says we have to check out of the hotel before noon.
   该职员说我们必须在中午前办理退房手续。
   If you check out after 12 noon, you'll have to pay for another day.
   如果你在中午 12 点后才退房,就必须多付一天的钱。

会话 A

1. **I have a reservation for a suite.** 我订了一间套房。
   我们在 Lesson 19 中已介绍过"make a reservation for..."(预订……)的用法,这里再介绍另一个常用的短语"have a reservation for..."。"have a reservation for..."是指"(已经)预订了……",强调的是预订的事实;而"make a reservation for..."则强调预订的动作。
   例 I have a reservation for a table for two.

我已经预订了一张两个人坐的餐桌。

A: Are you ready for your trip? 你的旅行准备好了吗?

B: I still have to make a reservation for the hotel. 我还得订旅馆。

* trip [trɪp] 名 旅行

2. **Please fill out this form.** 请填一下这张表格。

= Please <u>fill in</u> this form.

fill out (美式用法) 或 fill in (英式用法) 也是很实用的短语, 表示"填写 (表格、文件等)"的意思。

例 Before the job interview, you have to fill out an application form.

工作面试前, 你必须先填申请表。

* interview [ˈɪntəˌvju] 名 面谈
* application [ˌæpləˈkeʃən] 名 申请表 / 书

3. **Will you pay by cash or charge?** 您要付现金还是刷卡?

= Will you pay by cash or (by) credit card?

原句是由 "Will you pay by cash or by charge?" 省略而来。此处的 by charge 就是不付现金, 而用信用卡付账的意思, 也就等于 by credit card 之意。

* credit card [ˈkrɛdɪtˌkɑrd] 名 信用卡

例 I always pay for things by cash. 我买东西向来都是付现金。

It's very easy to overspend when you have a credit card.

当你有信用卡时就很容易花钱过度。

* overspend [ˈovəˈspɛnd] 动 花费过多

charge 除了用作名词外, 还可以作动词用, 表 "收费"、"索价" 之意。其句型如下:

charge + 人 + 金钱 + for + 物品

因某物向某人索取…… (金钱)的费用

例 The tutor charges his students US$1 an hour for English lessons.

那个家教教一个小时英文课向学生收 1 美元。

4. **Do you take traveler's checks?** 你们收旅行支票吗?

= Do you <u>accept</u> traveler's checks?

这里的 take 和 accept [əkˈsɛpt] 都是表 "接受" 的意思; 要询问

对方"接不接受……（的付款方式）"时，都可用"Do you take /
accept...?"表示。

例 A: Do you take credit cards? 你们收信用卡吗？

　　B: Sure. No problem. 当然收。没问题。

5. **Certainly.** 当然。

= Of course.

在对话中，用来回答对方表示"肯定"或"同意"别人的说法、看
法或请求、帮助时，就可用"Certainly."来回答，也就等于"Of
course."。

例 A: Do you have time to see me now? 你现在有空和我见面吗？

　　B: | Certainly.
　　　 | Of course.　当然有。

　　A: Can you help me fix my bike? 你能帮我修理自行车吗？

　　B: | Certainly.
　　　 | Of course.　当然可以。

　　A: May I use your phone? 我可以借用你的电话吗？

　　B: | Certainly.
　　　 | Of course.　当然可以。

会话 B

1. **One moment, please.** 请稍候 / 请稍等一下。

= One minute, please.

= Just a moment, please.

= Just a minute, please.

2. **You have a reservation for a single room, right?**

= You have a reservation for a single room, don't you?

您订了一间单人房，对不对？

此处的 right 就等于 don't you，表"对不对（呀）"的意思；这种在陈
述句之后加上 right 的用法（此时 right 的语气要上扬）称作反意疑
问句（又叫附加疑问句），这在英文中是很常见的。除了 right 之外，
这种反意疑问句的句型通常有五种，不过我们在介绍这五种句型
之前，要先知道形成反意疑问句的基本原则是：

肯定句要以否定反问；

否定句要以肯定反问；

而且反问部分的主语始终为人称代词（he、she、they、you、we...）。

a. 句中有 be 动词时，以该 be 动词形成反问。

> **例** 肯定句：John is nice, right? 约翰人很好，对不对？
>
> = John is nice, isn't he?
>
> 否定句：Tom and Mary aren't students, right?
>
> = Tom and Mary aren't students, are they?
>
> 汤姆和玛丽都不是学生，对吗？

b. 句中有助动词时，以该助动词形成反问。

> **例** 肯定句：You will come, right? 你会来，对不对？
>
> = You will come, won't you?
>
> 否定句：She can't speak English, right? 她不会说英文，对吗？
>
> = She can't speak English, can she?

c. 肯定句中有一般动词时，则按主语人称及动词时态，以 don't 或 doesn't 形成反问；否定句中因已有 do 或 does，故反问部分仍使用 do 或 does。

> **例** 肯定句：Helen loves flowers, right? 海伦很喜欢花，对不对？
>
> = Helen loves flowers, doesn't she?
>
> 否定句：You don't like me, right? 你不喜欢我，对吗？
>
> = You don't like me, do you?

d. 以 Let's（Let us 的缩写形式）引导的祈使句，其反意疑问句部分固定用 shall we。

> **例** Let's go to the movies tonight, shall we?
>
> 咱们今晚去看电影吧，好不好？

e. 以动词原形起首的祈使句，其反问部分固定用 will you。

> **例** Close the door, will you? 把门关上，好吗？

3. **Do you have any luggage?** 您有行李吗？

luggage 和 baggage [ˈbæɡɪdʒ] 都是表示"行李"的集合名词，而且都是不可数名词。因为"行李"包括旅行时所带的袋子、手提袋、手提箱、公文包等等，所以 luggage 和 baggage 是一种集合名称，因此就不能说 a luggage / baggage、two luggages / baggages...，但如果加上单位名称如 a piece of（一件……）时，我们就可以说 a piece of luggage / baggage（一件行李）、two pieces of luggage / baggage（两件行李）……。

例 I never take more than two pieces of luggage when I travel.

我旅行时从不会带超过两件以上的行李。

luggage 和 baggage 虽然是不可数名词，但组成行李的箱子、袋子等都是可数名词，这些常见的词有下列：

bag [bæg] 袋子

handbag [ˈhænd,bæg]（女用）手提包；手提袋

box [bɑks] 箱子

suitcase [ˈsut,kes] 手提箱

briefcase [ˈbrif,kes] 公文包

④ Substitution 替换

1. Mr. Brown will | check into the hotel / check in at the hotel | tomorrow.
布朗先生明天将在那家旅馆登记办理住宿手续。

2. I have a reservation for a | suite. 我订了一间套房。/ table for six. 我订了一张六个人坐的餐桌。

3. Please fill | out / in | this | form. / application.
请填一下这张表格 / 申请书。

4. Will you pay by cash or | charge? / credit card? | 您要付现金还是刷卡？

5. You have a reservation for a single room, | right? / don't you?
你订了一间单人房，对不对？

6. | Let's have lunch together, shall we? 咱们一起吃个午饭吧，要不要？/ Speak louder, will you? 说大声一点，好吗？

5　　*Exercises* 练习　　☾

I.　Use the right word: 请选出适当的单词:

doesn't	shall	by	are
piece	will	check	have

1.　The best time to _____ into a hotel is about 2 p.m.

2.　Excuse me, sir, but do you _____ a reservation?

3.　Can I pay _____ credit card?

4.　You aren't brothers, _____ you?

5.　Let's go home, _____ we?

6.　Shut up, _____ you?

7.　John likes Mary, _____ he?

8.　This _____ of luggage is really heavy.

II.　Complete the dialogue: 完成下列会话:

A: Excuse me. I have a reservation for a double room.

B: May I have your p_____?

A: H_____ you are.

B: You want the room for 3 days, d_____ you?

A: Yes. That's r_____.

B: Okay. Will you pay by cash or c_____?

A: Do you a_____ VISA cards?

B: Sure. Please just f_____ out this form.

Lesson 21

Changing Money
换钱

会话 A

A: I would like to cash these traveler's checks, please.

B: How much do you have?

A: Five hundred US dollars.

B: Do you have any identification?

A: Will my passport do?

B: That'll be fine.

A: 麻烦你，我想把这些旅行支票换成现金。

B: 你有多少？

A: 500 美元。

B: 你有什么身份证明文件吗？

A: 我的护照可以吗?

B: 那就可以了。

会话 B

A: What's the exchange rate for US dollars, please?

B: Which currency do you want to change your money into?

A: Hong Kong dollars, please.

B: It's 7.89 Hong Kong dollars to 1 US dollar.

A: Can you change US$100?

B: How do you want your money?

A: Seven hundreds, eight tens and the rest in change, please.

B: No problem.

A: 请问美元的汇率是多少?

B: 你要把钱换成哪一种货币?

A: 港币,麻烦你。

B: 汇率是 7.89 港币对 1 美元。

A: 你能换 100 美元吗?

B: 你要多少面额的钱?

A: 7 张 100 元, 8 张 10 元, 其余的换成零钱。

B: 没问题。

② *Vocabulary & Idioms* 单词短语注解

会话 A

1. **change** [tʃendʒ] 动（交）换

2. **cash** [kæʃ] 动 兑换现金 & 名 现金

3. **identification** [aɪˌdɛntəfəˈkeʃən] 名 身份证明（文件）

会话 B

1. **exchange rate** [ɪksˈtʃendʒˌret] 名（外汇）汇率

    exchange [ɪksˈtʃendʒ] 名 & 动 兑换；交换

    exchange A for B　把 A 换成 B

    exchange ＋ 物 ＋ with ＋ 人　和某人交换某物

    Could you please exchange this ten-dollar bill for two fives?

    可不可以请你把这张 10 块钱换成两个 5 块的呢？

    Would you like to exchange gifts with me?

    你愿不愿意和我交换礼物呢？

2. **currency** [ˈkɜənsɪ] 名 货币

3. **rest** [rɛst] 名 剩余（部分），其余

③ *Grammar Points* 语法重点

标题

1. **change money** 换钱

    有时亦可说 exchange money。

    change A into B　把 A 换成 B

    例 I want to change HK$30,000 into US dollars.

    我想把 30000 港币换成美金。

    * HK$30,000 的念法是 thirty thousand HK dollars 或 thirty thousand HK（HK dollars 是 Hong Kong dollars 的缩写）

会话 A

1. **I would like to cash these traveler's checks, please.**

   麻烦你, 我想把这些旅行支票换成现金。

   a. 此处的 cash 是动词, 表"兑换现金"的意思。

   例 Can you cash this check for me?

   你能帮我把这张支票兑换成现金吗?

   b. cash 也可作名词, 表"现金", 和 money、change (零钱) 一样,

   为不可数名词, 其用法和 change 一样有两种:

   例 How many cashes / changes do you have? (×)

   → How much cash / change do you have? (√)

   = How much do you have in cash / change?

   你有多少现金 / 零钱?

   I have 20 dollars in cash / change. 我有 20 元现金 / 零钱。

2. **Do you have any identification?** 你有任何身份证明文件吗?

   identification 是指证明身份的文件, 一般有三种证照可为证明:

   ID card = identity card [aɪˈdɛntətɪˌkɑrd] (身份证)

   driver's license [ˈdraɪvɚzˌlaɪsn̩s] (驾驶执照)

   passport [ˈpæsˌpɔrt] (护照)

3. **Will my passport do?** 我的护照可以吗?

   do 原表"做 (工作)", 此处则表"行"或"可以"。

   例 I do my homework every day. 我每天都做家庭作业。

   A: What would you like to drink? 你想喝点什么?

   B: Just water will do. 只要白开水就行了。

   A: Can you lend me some money? 你能借我一些钱吗?

   B: Will 100 dollars do? 100 块钱够不够?

4. **That'll be fine.** 那就可以了。

   = That'll be OK.

   = That'll do.

   例 A: Let's meet at 8 in the morning. Will it be too early for you?

   咱们早上 8 点碰面, 对你而言会不会太早?

B: No，that'll be fine. 不会，8 点可以。

A: OK，see you then. 好的，到时候见。

会话 B

1. **What's the exchange rate for US dollars, please?**
   请问美元的汇率是多少？

   What's the exchange rate for + 货币名称？
   某货币的汇率是多少？

   What's the exchange rate between + 货币名称 + and + 货币名称？
   某货币对某货币的汇率是多少？

   例 What's the exchange rate for the pound today?
   今天英镑的汇率是多少？

   * pound [paʊnd] 名 英镑

   What's the exchange rate between HK dollars and US dollars?
   港币对美金的汇率是多少？

2. **Which currency do you want to change your money into?**
   你要把钱换成哪一种货币？

   currency 是指某一国实际通用的货币而言。

   例 How much foreign currency do you have? 你有多少外币？

3. **It's 7.89 Hong Kong dollars to 1 US dollar.**
   汇率是 7.89 港币对 1 美元。

   7.89 的读法为 seven point eight nine。

   注意

   小数点之后的数字须一个一个分开念，不可合成十位数或百位
   数来念。如 18.18 须念成 eighteen point one eight，而不可念成
   eighteen point eighteen; 0.235 须念成 zero point two three five，不可
   念成 zero point two hundred and thirty-five。

4. **How do you want your money?** 你要多少面额的钱？
   本句为兑换外币时，银行柜员问顾客的话。比如说，你用港币换了
   350 美元，而美元有 1 元、5 元、10 元、20 元、50 元、100 元等面额不
   同的纸钞，要凑足 350 美元就会有各种不同的排列组合，所以柜员

会以此问句问你要如何分配。

5. **Seven hundreds, eight tens and the rest in change, please.**

= Seven one-hundred-dollar bills, eight ten-dollar bills and the rest in change, please.

7 张 100 元钞, 8 张 10 元钞, 其余的换成零钱。

bill [bɪl] 名 纸钞

此处的 the rest 为代词, 是 the rest of the money 之省略。

例 Only two students are absent, and the rest (of the students) are all present today.

今天只有两位学生缺席, 其余的均出席了。

* absent [ˈæbsn̩t] 形 缺席的
* present [ˈprɛzn̩t] 形 出席的

6. **No problem.** 没问题。

例 A: Can you kill Roger for me, James Bond?

B: No problem. He's a dead man.

A: 詹姆斯·邦德, 你能帮我把罗杰干掉吗?

B: 没问题, 他死定了。

---

④ *Substitution* 替换

1. I would like to cash | these traveler's checks, | please.
   | this check, |

   麻烦你, 我想把这些旅行支票 / 这张支票换成现金。

2. | Will my passport do? 我的护照可以吗?
   | That'll do. 那可以。
   | That won't do. 那不行。

3. What's the exchange rate
   | for US dollars, please?
   | between US dollars and Hong Kong dollars, please?
   请问美元的汇率是多少?
   请问美元对港币的汇率是多少?

4. How much do you have in | cash? / change? | 你有多少现金 / 零钱?

5. I have only ten dollars in | cash. / change. | 我只有10块现金 / 零钱。

5 *Exercises* 练习

I. Use the right word: 请选出适当的单词:

| rest | for | between | How |
| cash | do | change | identity |

1. I need some money. Fifty dollars will _____.
2. I need some _____ to make a phone call.
3. I would like to _____ this check, please.
4. Tom always carries his _____ card with him.
5. Do you want to exchange your toy gun _____ my model airplane?
6. What's the exchange rate _____ the Yen and US dollars?
7. _____ do you want your money?
8. I'll take these books; the _____ are for you.

II. Complete the dialogue: 完成下列会话:

A: Can you c_____ these traveler's checks for me, please?

B: Sure. I need some i_____, though.

A: OK. Here's my ID c_____.

B: That'll d_____. Which c_____ do you want your money in?

A: In US dollars, please.

B: No problem. That'll be twenty hundreds and the r_____ in tens, Okay?

A: That'll be f_____.

Lesson 22

Booking an Airline Ticket
订机票

1 *Dialogue* 会话

会话 A

A: Hi! My name is John Lin. I'd like to book a flight to Rome, please.

B: Do you wish to fly first class, business or economy?

A: Economy.

B: Date of departure?

A: July 4th.

B: OK. You're booked on flight number CX167. It departs at 11:15 AM.

A: 嗨！我叫林约翰。我想预订到罗马的班机。

B: 您想乘头等舱、商务舱还是经济舱？

A: 经济舱。

B: 出发的日期呢？

A: 7 月 4 日。

B: 好的。您预订的是 CX167 班机，早上 11 点 15 分起飞。

会话 B

A: Japan Airlines. Can I help you?

B: Yes. I'm Mr. Peter Lai. I'd like to reserve a round-trip ticket to Paris, please.

A: Which class? And for when?

B: Business class, for this Sunday.

A: One moment, please. ...OK. I've booked you on flight number 007. It departs at 5:30 p.m. Please call back on Friday to reconfirm.

B: OK.

A: Your confirmation code number is XE3849.

B: Thank you.

A: 日本航空公司。我可以为您效劳吗？

B: 是的。我是赖彼得先生。麻烦你，我想预订到巴黎的来回机票。

A: 您要什么舱位？还有是什么时候？

B: 商务舱，时间是这个星期天。

A: 请稍候。……好了，我已为您订了下午 5:30 起飞的 007

号班机。请在星期五打电话来再确认。

B: 好的。

A: 您的确认代码是 XE3849。

B: 谢谢。

2   *Vocabulary & Idioms* 单词短语注解

会话 A

1. **airline** [ˈɛrˌlaɪn] 名 航空公司

2. **Rome** [rom] 名 罗马(意大利首都)

3. **wish** [wɪʃ] 动 想(要), 希望

4. **fly** [flaɪ] 动 搭乘(飞机) & 动 飞(行)

5. **class** [klæs] 名 等级
   first class 头等舱

6. **business** [ˈbɪznɪs] 名 商业, 生意
   business class 二等舱, 商务舱

7. **economy** [ɪˈkɑnəmɪ] 名 经济
   economy class 经济舱

8. **departure** [dɪˈpɑrtʃɚ] 名 离开; 出发

9. **flight number** 班机号码

10. **depart** [dɪˈpɑrt] 动 出发

会话 B

1. **round-trip** [ˌraʊndˈtrɪp] 形 来回的, 往返的

2. **Paris** [ˈpærɪs] 名 巴黎(法国首都)

3. **reconfirm** [ˌrikənˈfɜm] 动 再确认

4. **confirmation** [ˌkɑnfəˈmeʃən] 名 确定, 确认
   confirmation code number 确认代码

3   *Grammar Points* 语法重点

会话 A

1. **Do you wish to fly first class, business or economy?**

= Do you wish to fly first class, business class or economy class?

您想乘头等舱、商务舱还是经济舱?

wish to + 动词　想要……

= hope to + 动词

* hope [hop] 动 希望

例 I wish to study abroad. 我想要出国念书。

= I hope to study abroad.

* abroad [ə'brɔd] 副 在国外

2.　**Date of departure?** 出发的日期呢?

= What's the date of your departure?

date 是指年、月、日等的"日期", date of departure 译作"出发日期";
"出生日期"的说法则为 date of birth; 但 date of birth 与 birthday 不
同的是：date of birth 包括出生的年、月、日, 而 birthday 则不包括出
生的年份。

例 If you tell me your date of birth, I'll know how old you are.

如果你告诉我你的出生日期, 我就知道你几岁了。

My birthday is December 25. 我的生日是 12 月 25 日。

3.　**It departs at 11:15 a.m.** 它起飞的时间是早上 11 点 15 分。

a.　depart 表"出发"、"离开", 除了单独使用外, 还可以与介词 for
连用, 形成下列用法：

depart for + 地方　出发 / 动身前往某地

例 The train departs on schedule every morning.

那班火车每天早上都按时出发。

* on schedule 按时;照时间表

schedule ['skɛdʒʊl] 名 时间 / 时刻表

Mr. Wang will depart for Hong Kong tomorrow.

王先生明天将动身前往香港。

b.　我们一般指确切的时间或时刻时, 前面通常都用介词 at 来表
示, 如：at ten（o'clock）（在 10 点钟）、at noon（在正午时, 约中
午 12 点）、at night（在晚上, 约 8、9 点以后）、at midnight（在午夜,
半夜 12 点）等。

例 Jimmy usually arrives at school at 6:30 am.

吉米通常早上 6 点半到校。

John goes to bed at midnight every day.

约翰每天到半夜才上床睡觉。

* go to bed　上床，就寝

　bed [bɛd]名 床

c.　如果要表示年、月、季节、上 / 下午及晚上时，那么前面的介词要用 in，如：in 2000（在 2000 年）、in March（在 3 月）、in spring（在春天）、in the morning（在早上）、in the afternoon（在下午）、in the night（在晚上，= at night）。

例 I will return to America in 2018. 我将在 2018 年回美国。

* return [rɪˈtɜn]动 返回，归来

　Mr. Li works best in the morning.

　李先生上午的工作效率最高。

d.　表日期或星期几时，介词则须用 on 来表示，如：on July 4（在 7 月 4 日）、on Christmas（在圣诞节，即 12 月 25 日）、on Sunday（在星期日）。

例 He'll come on February 29. 他会在 2 月 29 号那天来。

　I have to go to church on Sunday. 这个星期天我必须上教堂。

* church [tʃɜtʃ]名 教堂

会话 B

1.　**I'd like to reserve a round-trip ticket to Paris, please.**

= I'd like to book a round-trip ticket to Paris，please.

麻烦你，我想预订到巴黎的来回机票。

a round-trip ticket 来回票

a one-way ticket 单程票

* one-way [ˌwʌnˈwe]形 单程的；单向的，单行的

这里的 round-trip 及 one-way 都是形容词，round-trip 是指"往返的"、"来回旅行的"；one-way 则是指"单程 / 向 / 行的"，如：one-way street（单行道）。

例 How much is it for a round-trip ticket to Los Angeles?

到洛杉矶的来回票要多少钱?

I will buy a one-way ticket to New York because I don't intend to return.

我要买一张到纽约的单程票,因为我不打算回来了。

* intend [ɪnˈtɛnd] 动 打算

You can't drive in there; it's a one-way street.

你不能开进那里;那条是单行道。

* drive [draɪv] 动 开车

2. **Which class? And for when?**

= Which class would you like to fly? And when do you want to leave?

您要搭乘哪一种舱位? 还有您要什么时候离开?

3. **I've booked you on flight number 007.**

= I have booked you on flight number 007.

我已为您订了 007 号班机。

动词 book(预订 = reserve [rɪˈzɜv])之后,除了可以接旅馆房间、座位、门票等,还可以接"人"作宾语,表示"为某人预订……"的意思。

例 I'd like to book a room for three nights.

我想订一个房间住三个晚上。

Please book me on the next flight to Canada.

请帮我订下一班到加拿大的班机。

The secretary books Mr. Li in at the Hilton hotel every time he travels abroad.

每次李先生出国,秘书都会帮他预订希尔顿饭店的房间。

* secretary [ˈsɛkrəˌtɛrɪ] 名 秘书

4. **Please call back on Friday to reconfirm.**

请在星期五打电话来再确认。

我们一般在预订班机时,为避免机位被取消,都还要在出发前 3 天打电话给航空公司再做确认,以确保机位。

例 To be safe, I always reconfirm my flight three days before the flight.

为了保险起见,我都会在 3 天前再确认我的班机。

4   *Substitution* 替换

1. I $\begin{vmatrix} \text{wish} \\ \text{hope} \end{vmatrix}$ to travel around the world. 我希望能够环游世界。

2. Mr. Wang will $\begin{vmatrix} \text{depart} \\ \text{leave} \end{vmatrix}$ for Hong Kong tomorrow.
王先生明天将动身前往香港。

3. John goes to bed at $\begin{vmatrix} \text{midnight} \\ \text{ten (o'clock)} \end{vmatrix}$ every day.
约翰每天都到半夜才上床睡觉。
约翰每天都在 10 点钟上床睡觉。

4. Mr. Li works best $\begin{vmatrix} \text{in the morning.} \\ \text{in the afternoon.} \\ \text{at night.} \end{vmatrix}$
李先生上午 / 下午 / 晚上的工作效率最好。

5. Peter will come on $\begin{vmatrix} \text{February 29.} \\ \text{Christmas Day.} \end{vmatrix}$
彼得会在 2 月 29 号 / 圣诞节（12 月 25 号）那天来。

6. How much is it for a $\begin{vmatrix} \text{round-trip} \\ \text{one-way} \end{vmatrix}$ ticket to Los Angeles?
到洛杉矶的来回票 / 单程票要多少钱？

5   *Exercises* 练习

I. Use the right word: 请选出适当的单词：

birthday	wish	book	at
departs	on	reconfirm	birth

1. I do not _____ to see you here when I return.
2. Your date of _____ is January 30, 1970.
3. The train _____ on time, so you must not be late.
4. School begins _____ September 1 every year.
5. Dad works _____ night and sleeps during the day.
6. Can you _____ me in at the Lai Lai Sheraton, please?

7. Jack's _____ is June 6.

8. Do I have to _____ my return flight when I arrive in Tokyo?

II. Complete the dialogue: 完成下列会话 :

A: Excuse me. My name is John Smith. I'd like to r_____ my flight back to Taiwan.

B: Which c_____ are you booked in?

A: The e_____ class.

B: And what is the f_____ number?

A: It's XE707.

B: Oh, yes. You're booked to leave o_____ Sunday, right?

A: That's right. The flight is a_____ 8 p.m., right?

B: Right. It d_____ at that time, so you'll have to be there about an hour before 8 p.m.

Lesson 23

At the Airport I

在机场（一）

会话 A

A: This is the arrival lounge.

B: I know. Where is the departure lounge?

A: Come. Follow me.

B: There! The check-in counters are over there.

A: Don't we have to go pay the airport tax first?

B: No. We pay it after we check in.

A: 这里是入境大厅。

B: 我知道。出境大厅在哪里呢？

A: 来吧，跟我走。

B: 那里！办理登机手续的柜台在那里。

A: 我们不用先去付机场税吗?

B: 不用。先办完登机手续后再付。

会话 B

A: Good morning. May I have your passport, please?

B: Here you are.

A: Smoking or non-smoking?

B: Non-smoking.

A: Aisle or window seat?

B: Window seat, please.

A: Do you have any luggage to check in?

B: Yes. This is my carry-on luggage and I'll check in these two suitcases.

A: 早上好。请把您的护照给我好吗?

B: 在这儿。

A: 您要坐在吸烟区或非吸烟区?

B: 非吸烟区。

A: 您要靠走道还是靠窗的座位?

B: 请给我靠窗的座位。

A: 您有什么行李要托运吗?

B: 有的。这是我的随身行李,这两个行李箱我要托运。

2 *Vocabulary & Idioms* 单词短语注解

会话 A

1. **airport** [ˈɛrˌpɔrt] 名 机场

2. **arrival lounge** [əˈraɪvlˌlaundʒ] 名 (机场) 入境大厅

3. **departure lounge** [dɪˈpartʃəˌlaundʒ] 名 (机场) 出境大厅

4. **follow** [ˈfɑlo] 动 跟随

5. **check-in counter** [ˈtʃɛkˌɪnˌkauntə] 名 办理登机手续的柜台
   counter [ˈkauntə] 名 柜台

6. **pay** [pe] 动 付 (钱)

7. **tax** [tæks] 名 税

会话 B

1. **aisle** [aɪl] 名 通道, 走道

2. **window** [ˈwɪndo] 名 窗 (户)

3. **seat** [sit] 名 座位
   Take a seat, please. (较客气)
   = Sit down, please. 请坐。

4. **carry-on** [ˈkærɪˌɑn] 形 随身携带的

3 *Grammar Points* 语法重点

会话 A

1. **This is the arrival lounge.** 这里是入境大厅。
   a. arrival [əˈraɪvl] 名 到达
      例 The fans are waiting for the arrival of the movie star.
        影迷们正在等那位影星抵达。
      arrive [əˈraɪv] 动 到达
      例 When will the plane arrive? 这班飞机何时到达?

注意

arrive 之后常接介词 at 或 in 再接地方名词, 如下列用法:

arrive at + 地点 (建筑物如邮局、车站等)

到达……

arrive in + 地方 (大地方如城市、国家等)

到达……

例 They will arrive at the hotel before six o'clock.

他们将在 6 点前到达旅馆。

The plane will arrive in New York tonight.

这班飞机今晚将抵达纽约。

b. arrival lounge 入境大厅

departure lounge 出境大厅

上列两个大厅皆在机场航站楼 (air terminal [ˈɛrˌtɜˈmənḷ]) 里面。

lounge [laundʒ] 是大厅或休息室的意思, 如 teacher's lounge (教师休息室), 但旅馆或饭店内的大厅则叫作 lobby [ˈlabɪ]。

2. **Come. Follow me.** 来吧, 跟我走。

follow me 表"跟我走", 在口语对话中就等于 this way。

例 A: Where can I find the bathroom? 洗手间在哪里?

B: Follow me. (= This way.) 跟我来。

3. **There! The check-in counters are over there.**

那里! 办理登机手续的柜台在那里。

a. check-in counter 指办理报到手续的柜台, 在机场办理的是登机手续; 在旅馆则是办理住宿登记的手续。

b. over there 在那里

over here 在这里

上列中 over 为作强调用的副词。over there / here 为目视距离内的指示用法, 通常亦可在其前加上另一个强调副词 right, 形成 right over there (就在那里) 和 right over here (就在这里)。此外, 亦可将 over 省略, 形成 right there / here, 但此时则无距离的含意。

例 Who is the man standing over there?

站在那里的那位男子是谁呢?

The thing we are looking for is <u>right over here</u>.

我们所要找的东西就在这里。

I will be <u>right here</u> waiting for you. 我将在这里等你。

注意

right 亦可用来强调介词短语, over 则不可。

例 There's a beautiful fountain right in the middle of the park.

在公园的正中央有一座漂亮的喷水池。

* fountain [ˈfaʊntn̩]名 喷水池, 喷泉

4. **Don't we have to <u>go pay</u> the airport tax first?**

= Don't we have to <u>go and pay</u> the airport tax first?

我们不用先去付机场税吗?

a. 英文中两个动词同在一个句子时, 必须有连词连接,否则为错误句型。但 go 和 come 以动词原形出现时,则可将其后的连词 and 省略, 直接加另一个动词。

例 They sing, dance happily day after day. (×)

→ They sing <u>and</u> dance happily day after day. (√)

日复一日他们快乐地唱歌和跳舞。

Please go <u>and</u> buy me a newspaper. 请去帮我买一份报纸。

= Please <u>go buy</u> me a newspaper.

When you have time, come <u>and</u> visit me.

= When you have time, <u>come visit</u> me.

有时间的时候,请来看我。

b. pay 为动词, 表"付(钱)"的意思,下列为常见的用法:

pay + 钱 + for... 付钱买……

pay sb + 钱 + for... 为……付钱给某人

例 I will not pay one hundred dollars for the toy.

我不会付 100 块买这个玩具。

She pays me a lot of money for doing this work.

她付我很多钱做这个工作。

c. the airport tax 机场税

政府向人民征收机场税以回收建造机场的费用。

d. first 此处表"首先"之意,可置于句首或句尾;置于句首时可
等于 first of all,但置于句尾时,则不可用 first of all 取代。亦即
first of all 只能置于句首。

例 A: What can I do to make my English better?

B: | First, | you have to get a good dictionary.
   | First of all, |

A: 我要怎么做才能使我的英文变好?

B: 首先,你必须要有一本好词典。

5. **We pay it after we check in.** 我们先办完登机手续后再付。

我们在 Lesson 20 中已学过 check in 乃指(在旅馆)办理住宿的手续;
但此处的 check in 则指(在机场)办理登机的手续而言。

会话 B

1. **May I have your passport, please?** 请把您的护照给我好吗?

May I have your..., please? 请把您的……给我好吗?

这是很客气的要求,your 之后可接各种名词。

例 May I have your attention, please? The plane will take off in five
minutes.

各位请注意,飞机将于 5 分钟后起飞。

* take off (飞机等) 起飞,升空

2. **Smoking or non-smoking?** 你要坐在吸烟区或非吸烟区?

= Would you like to sit in the smoking section or the non-smoking section?
以前飞机上分吸烟区和非吸烟区。近年来考虑到飞行安全，大部分飞机上都全面禁烟，空乘员会作类似下列广播：

Ladies and gentlemen, this is a non-smoking flight. Please do not smoke during the flight. Thanks for your cooperation.
各位女士和先生，本次班机禁烟，请不要在飞行期间抽烟，谢谢您的合作。

 * cooperation [ko͵ɑpəˈreʃən] 名 合作

3. **Aisle or window seat?** 您要靠走道的座位还是靠窗的座位?

= Would you like an aisle seat or a window seat?
aisle seat 是指在飞机上或火车上等靠走道的座位，而 window seat 是指靠窗户的座位。

4. **Do you have any luggage to check in?** 您有什么行李要托运吗?

    a. luggage [ˈlʌgɪdʒ] 名 行李

    = baggage [ˈbægɪdʒ] 名

    注意

    上列为集合名词，是不可数名词，不可说 a luggage / baggage、two luggages / baggages、many luggages / baggages...，而须说 a piece of luggage / baggage（一件行李）、two pieces of luggage / baggage（二件行李）、a lot of luggage / baggage（很多行李）。
    所谓集合名词是指任何同类东西总称的名词，例如 handbag（手提袋）、suitcase（行李箱），它们是可数的普通名词，可说 a handbag、two handbags、a suitcase、two suitcases，但总称为 luggage 或 baggage（行李）。其他如 a dollar（1 美元）、a cent（1 分钱）亦为可数的普通名词，但总称为 money（钱）时，就变成不可数的集合名词，不可说成 a money、two moneys。类似的集合名词如 trash [træʃ]、garbage [ˈgɑrbɪdʒ]、rubbish [ˈrʌbɪʃ] 均为“垃圾”之意，news [njuz] 表示“消息”, information [͵ɪnfəˈmeʃən] 表示“信息”, furniture [ˈfɜnɪtʃɚ] 表示“家具”等，为数并不多，只要稍加留意即可。

    b. 此处的“check in...”乃指办理行李由飞机托运的手续。

4 *Substitution* 替换

1. This is the $\begin{vmatrix} \text{arrival} \\ \text{departure} \end{vmatrix}$ lounge. 这里是入境 / 出境大厅。

2. Jack usually arrives at the school at seven o'clock.
   Rose will arrive in Taipei tomorrow.
   杰克通常 7 点到校。
   罗丝明天将抵达台北。

3. Follow me. 跟我来。
   This way.

4. The check-in counters are $\begin{vmatrix} \text{over there.} \\ \text{right over there.} \end{vmatrix}$
   办理登机手续的柜台在那里 / 就在那里。

5. Don't we have to go pay the airport tax first?
   My friends and I will go see a movie tonight.
   我们不用先去付机场税吗?
   我和我朋友今晚要去看电影。

6. May I have your $\begin{vmatrix} \text{passport,} \\ \text{coat,} \end{vmatrix}$ please? 请把你的护照给我好吗?
   请把你的外套给我好吗?

5 *Exercises* 练习

I. Use the right word: 请选出适当的单词:

seat	pieces	First	for
in	at	right	go

1. The plane will arrive _____ the airport on time.

2. It hurts _____ here, doctor.

3. Please _____ pick up the clothes at the laundromat.

4. Please take a _____.

5. Our boss will arrive _____ Tokyo tomorrow morning.

6. You can check in two _____ of luggage.

7. _____ of all, you must fill out this form.

8. Uncle Paul pays me US$100 _____ teaching my cousin English.

II. Complete the dialogue: 完成下列会话:

A: May I h_____ your passport, please?

B: Sure. Here you are. Do I have to pay the airport tax f_____?

A: No. You can pay it later.

B: Okay. Can I have a w_____ seat, please?

A: In the smoking or non-smoking s_____?

B: Non-smoking, please.

A: Any l_____ to check in?

B: Just this big one o_____ here.

A: I see.

Lesson 24

At the Airport II
在机场（二）

1   *Dialogue* 会话

会话 A

A: Please fill out these tags and attach them to your suitcases. Then put them on the scale.

B: OK.

A: I'm afraid your luggage is overweight. You'll have to pay an excess baggage charge.

B: How much will that be?

A: Let me see—US$10.

B: That's not too bad.

A: 请填好这些标签后把它们系在你的行李箱上。然后把它们放在秤上。

B: 好的。

A: 恐怕您的行李超重了。您必须额外付行李超重费。

206

B: 那要多少钱？

A: 让我看看—— 10 美元。

B: 还不算太糟。

会话 B

A: Here are your tickets. The baggage claim stubs are attached to them.

B: Thank you.

A: And here is your boarding pass. You board at Gate 12.

B: OK. Is that all?

A: No. Please wait here till your luggage goes through the X-ray machine.

B: OK.

A: Have a nice flight.

B: Thank you.

A: 这里是您的机票。领取行李的存根就附在上面。

B: 谢谢。

A: 这儿是您的登机牌。您在 12 号口登机。

B: 好的。就这样吗？

A: 还没。请在这里等您的行李通过 X 光检测机。

B: 好吧。

A: 祝您乘机愉快。

B: 谢谢。

2 **Vocabulary & Idioms** 单词短语注解 ✍

会话 A

1. **tag** [tæg] 名 标签

2. **attach** [əˈtætʃ] 动 系, 固定

3. **put** [pʊt] 动 放, 摆

4. **scale** [skel] 名 秤, 磅秤

5. **overweight** [ˈovəˌwet] 形 超 / 过重的

6. **excess** [ɪkˈsɛs] 形 额外的; 超过的

会话 B

1. **baggage claim stub**　提领行李的存根
   claim [klem] 名 (对某事物的) 要求权, 所有权
   stub [stʌb] 名 存根, 票根

2. **boarding pass** [ˈbɔrdɪŋˌpæs] 名 登机牌

3. **board** [bɔrd] 动 登上(飞机、船等)

4. **gate** [get] 名 大门

5. **wait** [wet] 动 等(待)

6. **till** [tɪl] 连 直到……为止

7. **X-ray machine** [ˈɛksˈre məˌʃin] 名 X 光检测机

3 **Grammar Points** 语法重点 〰

会话 A

1. **Please fill out these tags and attach them to your suitcases.**
   请填好这些标签后把它们系在你的行李箱上。
   a.　fill out...　填写……
   ＝　fill in...

例 Please fill out this form and give it to me.
请填写这份表格然后交给我。

b. attach 是动词，表"缚、系"、"固定"的意思，该词常与介词 to 连用，形成下列用法：

attach A to B　把 A 系在 / 到 B 上

例 He attaches the string to his kite. 他把绳子系在风筝上。

* string [strɪŋ] 名 绳子
　 kite [kaɪt] 名 风筝

2. **I'm afraid your luggage is overweight.** 恐怕你的行李超重了。

= I'm afraid that your luggage is overweight.

a. I'm afraid + that + 主语 + 动词　恐怕……
上列句型中 that 常被省略。

例 I'm afraid (that) it is going to rain this afternoon.
恐怕今天下午会下雨。

b. overweight 是形容词，表"超重的"之意。

人 + be overweight 某人体重过重

例 Anyone can see that you're overweight; you should go on a diet.
任何人都看得出来你体重过重，你应该节食了。

* go on a diet [ˈdaɪət] 节食

3. **You'll have to pay an excess baggage charge.**
你必须额外付行李超重费。

a. 注意 have to 和 must 的区别：
have to 和 must 虽然都可译为"必须"，但 have to 是含有被勉强而不得不的意味，而 must 则除此意之外，尚有道德上不得不的意味。

例 You ⎰have to⎱ do this work whether you like it or not.
　　 ⎰must ⎱
不管你喜不喜欢，你都必须做这工作。

We must love our country. 我们必须爱国。

b. excess baggage charge（超重行李费）就是超过免费行李限额部分，要另外付的运费。

4. **How much will that be?** 那要多少钱?

购物时，不论你买多少样东西，加总后得到的价钱，总额是一个数字，故代词用 that。

例 A: How much will that be? 总共是多少钱?

B: That will be 50 dollars in all. 总共是 50 元。

5. **Let me see—US$10.** 让我看看—— 10 美元。

let me see 或 let's see 之后常接破折号 (——)，表示停顿之意，说话者此时可能是在计算、想或思考等。

例 A: How long are you going to stay here?

B: Let me see / Let's see — five days, I think.

A: 你打算在这里停留多久?

B: 让我看看——我想是 5 天吧。

6. **That's not too bad.** 那还不算太糟。

That's too bad! 太可惜了!

= What a shame!

* shame [ʃem] 名 遗憾

例 A: How much money have you lost? 你丢了多少钱?

B: Only five dollars. 5 块钱而已。

A: That's not too bad, is it? 那还不算太糟, 不是吗?

A: I'm afraid I can't go to your party tonight.

B: Oh, | that's too bad! |
　　 | what a shame! |

A: 恐怕我今晚不能去参加你的派对。

B: 哦, 太可惜了!

会话 B

1. **Here are your tickets. The baggage claim stubs are attached to them.**

这里是你的机票, 领取行李的存根就附在上面。

a. Here is + 单数名词　这里是……

Here are + 复数名词　这里是……

例 A: Here is a little gift for you. 这是送你的一份小礼物。

B: Oh, thank you so much! 哦，真是太感谢你了！

Here are the cookies I like. 这些是我喜欢的饼干。

* cookie [ˈkʊkɪ] 名 饼干

b. baggage claim stub 是指提领行李的存根，此处的 claim 是名词，但 claim 也可以作动词用，表 "提领（行李）" 的意思。

例 Where can I claim my baggage? 我要去哪里提领我的行李呢？

2. And here is your boarding pass. You board at Gate 12.

= And here is your boarding pass. You board at Gate Number 12.

这儿是你的登机牌，你在 12 号口登机。

a. boarding pass（登机牌）是在机场柜台登记上飞机后，地勤人员会给旅客一张允许登机的证件，上面有座位号码、登机口号码等数据，是登机时的重要证件。

b. board 是动词，表示 "登上（飞机、火车、巴士、船等公共交通工具）" 之意。

例 Flight 251 for Singapore is now boarding at Gate 10.

飞往新加坡的 251 次班机正在 10 号口登机。

Passengers should board the train now. 旅客们现在该上火车了。

3. Is that all? 就这样吗？

例 A: Your mother wants me to tell you that you have to go home before 10 o'clock.

B: Is that all?

A: 你母亲要我告诉你，你必须在 10 点以前回家。

B: 就这样吗？

A: Please buy me a paper, a beer and a pack of cigarettes.

B: Is that all?

A: 请帮我买一份报纸、一瓶啤酒和一包香烟。

B: 就这样吗？

4. Please wait here till your luggage goes through the X-ray machine.

请在这里等你的行李通过 X 光检测机。

a. till (= until [ən'tɪl]) 可作连词，之后接主语和动词；亦可作介词，之后接名词作宾语。

> 例 They will not leave | till | the sun goes down.
> | until |

> 他们直到太阳下山才会离开。

> I'll stay here | till | Friday. 我将一直待到这个礼拜五。
> | until |

b. go through... 通过……

> 例 She is afraid to go through dark alleys at night.

> 她害怕在晚上通过黑暗的巷道。

> * alley ['ælɪ]名 小巷

5. **Have a nice flight.** 祝乘机愉快。

= May you have a nice flight.

= I hope (that) you (may) have a nice flight.

由上列等句中，大家不难看出"Have a nice flight."的简化过程。其他如"Have a good time."（祝你玩得愉快。）或"Have a nice day."（祝你今天过得愉快。）等，其简化过程亦如上列。

4 **Substitution** 替换

1. I'm afraid | your luggage is overweight. 恐怕你的行李超重了。
   | I have to leave now. 恐怕我现在必须离开了。

2. You | have to / must | finish the job by twelve o'clock.
   你必须在 12 点前完成这项工作。

3. | That's too bad! 太可惜了!
   | What a shame!

4. | Here are your tickets. 这里是你的机票 / 书。
   | Here is your book.

5. You board at | Gate 12. 你在 12 号口登机。
   | Gate Number 12.

6. Please wait here | till / until | your luggage goes through the X-ray machine.
   请在这里等你的行李通过 X 光检测机。

7. | Have a nice flight. 祝你乘机愉快。
   | May you have a nice flight.
   | I hope (that) you (may) have a nice flight.

5 **Exercises** 练习

I. Use the right word: 请选出适当的单词 :

see	has	all	bad
must	out	to	that

1. To apply for a driver's license, you must fill _____ this application form.

2. Please attach this tag _____ your luggage.

3. I'm afraid _____ I won't be able to get up on time.

4. Parents _____ take care of their children.

5. Bill _____ to play very well to win the game.

6. Let's _____ —— I think I have enough money for lunch.

7. I have to pay US$10. Is that _____?

8. My grandfather's health is not too _____.

II.   Complete the dialogue: 完成下列会话 :

A: Please put your luggage on the s _____. Wow! I'm afraid they're too heavy. You've got to pay an excess baggage c _____.

B: How much will t _____ be?

A: Let me s _____ — US$20.

B: Here you are.

A: Here are your baggage c _____ stubs and your boarding p _____.

B: So I should go t _____ Gate 5.

A: That's right. Have a nice f _____.

Lesson 25

At the Post Office
在邮局

Dialogue 会话

会话 A

A: I'd like to register this letter, please.

B: Where to?

A: Los Angeles.

B: OK. Let me weigh it. That'll be three dollars, please.

A: Here you are. Do I have to fill out a form?

B: No. Just give me your name, address and telephone number.

A: 麻烦你，我想用挂号寄这封信。

B: 寄到哪里？

A: 洛杉矶。

B: 好的，让我来称一下重量。邮资是3美元，麻烦您。

A: 拿去吧。我必须填写表格吗？

B: 不必。只要把您的姓名、住址和电话给我就行了。

会话 B

A: I'd like to send this by air mail, please.

B: Is it a birthday card?

A: Yes. Why do you ask?

B: Cards are cheaper than letters.

A: Oh! Really?

B: You can't seal the envelope, though.

A: OK. How much for the stamps?

B: Two dollars.

A: 我想要用航空邮寄这个，麻烦你。

B: 那是生日贺卡吗？

A: 是的。你为什么这样问？

B: 卡片比信件便宜一些。

A: 哦！真得吗？

B: 不过您不能把信封封起来。

A: 好吧。我要贴多少钱的邮票？

B: 2 美元。

2 Vocabulary & Idioms 单词短语注解

会话 A

1. **post office** [ˈpost ˌɔfɪs] 名 邮局
2. **register** [ˈrɛdʒɪstə] 动 挂号邮寄
3. **letter** [ˈlɛtə] 名 信
4. **weigh** [we] 动 称……的重量
5. **address** [ˈædrɛs / əˈdrɛs] 名 地址

会话 B

1. **send** [sɛnd] 动 寄；发出
2. **air mail** [ˈɛrˌmel] 名 航空邮件
3. **card** [kɑrd] 名 卡片
   birthday card   生日卡片
4. **seal** [sil] 动 封；密封
5. **envelope** [ˈɛnvəˌlop] 名 信封
6. **though** [ðo] 副 不过，然而
7. **stamp** [stæmp] 名 邮票

3 Grammar Points 语法重点

标题

at the post office 在邮局
in the post office 在邮局里面
注意这里用 at 和 in 的区别：
用 at 时，表示在某栋建筑物的里面或外面并不一定；而用 in 时则强调是在建筑物的里面。
例 I'll meet you at the station. 我将在车站和你碰面。

217

比较：

I'll meet you in the station. 我将在车站里面和你碰面。

会话 A

1. **I'd like to register this letter, please.**

   麻烦你，我想用挂号寄这封信。

   register this letter 用挂号寄这封信

   例 A: Do you want to register this letter? 这封信你要寄挂号吗？

   B: Yes, please. 是的，麻烦你。

2. **Where to?** 您要把信寄到哪里？

   = Where do you want to send this letter?

   "Where to?"为口语上简洁的问句，通常是"Where are you going?"（你要去哪里？）的意思，但此处是表"你要把信寄到哪里？"。

   注意

   "Where are you going?"不可说成"Where are you going to?"因为 where 是副词，修饰 going，不能作 to 的宾语，但简略成口语用法时，则说"Where to?"。

   例 A: I'm getting out of here. 我要离开这里。

   B: Where to? / Where are you going? 到哪去？ / 你要去哪里？

   A: Out for some fresh air. 出去呼吸些新鲜空气。

3. **Let me weigh it.** 让我来称一下它的重量。

   a. Let + 人 + 动词 让某人……

   例 Let him do it alone. 让他自己一个人做。

   b. weigh 是动词，表"称……的重量"的意思。

   例 Do you often weigh yourself? 你时常量体重吗？

4. **That'll be three dollars, please.** 邮资是 3 美元，麻烦你。

   a. That'll be + 金钱 是 / 要……（钱）

   That'll 是 That will 的缩写。

   例 A: How much is it? 那个要多少钱？

   B: That'll be twenty dollars. 那要 20 美元。

   b. please 表示"请"，是客气礼貌的用词，可置于句首、句尾或句中使用。

例 Sit down, please. 请坐。

= Please sit down.

Open the door, please. 请把门打开。

= Please open the door.

Would you please do me a favor? 可不可以请你帮我一个忙？

* Would you please + 动词？ 可不可以请你……？

5. **Do I have to fill out a form?** 我必须填写表格吗？

fill out a form 填写表格

fill in a form

例 Please fill out / in the form in detail. 请详细填写这份表格。

* detail [ˈditel]名 细节（in detail 表示"详细地"）

会话 B

1. **I'd like to send this by air mail, please.**

我想要用航空邮寄这个，麻烦你。

by air mail	寄空运
by sea mail	寄海运
by regular mail	寄平信
by registered mail	寄挂号
by special delivery	寄特快专递

= by express delivery

例 It's cheaper to send a package by sea mail than by air mail.

用海运寄包裹比寄空运便宜。

I want to send the letter by special delivery.

= I want to send the letter by express delivery.

我要用限时专送寄这封信。

注意

mail [mel]名 邮件 & 动 邮寄

mail 作名词时，表各种邮件的总称（包括信及包裹），为不可数名词；作动词时表"邮寄"。

mail a letter 寄一封信

= send a letter

= post a letter

例 I usually receive many mails every day. (×)

→ I usually receive a lot of mail every day. (√)

通常我每天都会收到很多邮件。

Please mail the letter for me. 请帮我寄这封信。

= Please send the letter for me.

= Please post the letter for me.

2. **You can't seal the envelope, though.**

不过你不能把信封封起来。

a. seal 是动词，表"(密)封"的意思。

例 Seal the letter before you mail it. 寄信之前要把信封好。

b. though 有下列两种重要用法：

（1）作副词，表"不过、然而"，使用时通常置于句尾，前面加逗号。

＊本句的"You can't seal the envelope, though."即为此种用法。

例 A: Can I borrow your bike?

B: Yes, you can. Don't break it, though.

A: 我可以向你借自行车吗？

B: 是的，可以。不过别把它弄坏哦。

（2）作连词，表"虽然"，通常置于句首。但要注意的是：中文的句法有"虽然……，但是……"的习惯用法，但英文中却不能用"Though..., but..."的句型，因为 though 和 but 都是连词，依英文语法规则，一句中只能有一个连词，故用 though 就不能再用 but。相同的情形亦发生在"因为……，所以……"的句法，英文中不能用"Because..., so..."的句法，而只能用其一。

例 Though he is nice, but I don't like him. (×)

→ Though he is nice, I don't like him. (√)

= He is nice, but I don't like him.

虽然他人很好,但是我不喜欢他。

Because he is nice, so I like him. (✕)

→ Because he is nice, I like him. (✓)

= He is nice, so I like him. (✓)

因为他人很好,所以我喜欢他。

4 Substitution 替换

1. I'll meet you | at the restaurant. | 我将和你在餐厅碰面。
   | in the restaurant. | 我将和你在餐厅里面碰面。

2. Let me weigh it. | 让我来称一下它的重量。
   Let me help you. | 让我帮你吧。

3. Would you please | do me a favor? | 可不可以请你帮我一个忙?
   | open the door for me? | 可不可以请你帮我开个门?

4. I'd like to send this by | air mail,
   | sea mail,
   | regular mail, | please.
   | registered mail,
   | special delivery,

   我想要用航空 / 海运 / 平信 / 挂号 / 限时专送邮寄这个, 麻烦你。

5. Though he is rich, he is very stingy.
   He is rich, but he is very stingy.
   虽然他很有钱,但他却很吝啬。

6. Because I am busy, I can't go with you.
   I am busy, so I can't go with you.
   因为我很忙, 所以我不能跟你去。

5 Exercises 练习

I. Use the right word: 请选出适当的单词 :

cheaper	for	Though	but
mail	special	please	Because

1. Would you _____ carry this heavy box for me?

2. I'd like to send this letter by _____ delivery, please.

3. Do you have much _____ every day?

4. If you're going to the post office, can you mail this letter _____ me?

5. This bike is _____ than that one.

6. _____ he is old, he is very healthy.

7. _____ Tom is kind, he has many friends.

8. Jack is handsome, _____ Mary doesn't like him.

II. Complete the dialogue: 完成下列会话：

A: I'd like to send this letter b_____ air mail, please.

B: I'll have to w_____ it.

A: Okay. H_____ much is it?

B: Thirty US. Would you like to r_____ the letter?

A: But regular mail is c_____, isn't it?

B: Of course. It's safer, t_____.

A: But it'll be more expensive, right?

B: Okay. I understand. T_____ will be US$30, please.

Lesson 26

At the Doctor's

看病

会话 A

A: Doctor, I think I have the flu.

B: Do you have a cough, too?

A: No. Not really.

B: Do you have a sore throat?

A: A little. But I have a bit of a fever.

B: OK. Let me have a look.

A: 医生，我想我得了流行性感冒。

B: 你也咳嗽吗？

A: 不，算不上真的咳嗽。

B: 喉咙会痛吗？

A: 一点点。但我有一点发烧。

B: 好的。让我来看看。

会话 B

A: Open your mouth and say, "Ah..."

B: Ah...

A: Yes. It's quite serious. I think you need a shot.

B: Is it going to hurt?

A: Don't worry. It'll soon be over.

B: Ouch!

A: OK. It's done. Also, take these pills 3 times a
day after meals.

B: OK. Thanks, doctor. Bye.

A: 张开嘴巴说"啊……"。

B: 啊……。

A: 是了,情况相当严重。我想你得打一针。

B: 会不会痛呢?

A: 别担心,很快就会结束的。

B: 哎唷!

A: 好了,打完针了。还有,饭后服用这些药丸,一天三次。

B: 好的。谢谢你,医生。再见。

② *Vocabulary & Idioms* 单词短语注解 ✍

会话 A

1. **doctor** [ˈdɑktɚ] 名 医生
   at the doctor's 在医生诊疗室
   = at the doctor's office

2. **flu** [flu] 名 流行性感冒

3. **cough** [kɔf] 名 咳嗽

4. **sore** [sɔr] 形 (疼)痛的

5. **throat** [θrot] 名 喉咙

6. **fever** [ˈfivɚ] 名 发烧

会话 B

1. **mouth** [mauθ] 名 嘴，口

2. **ah** [ɑ] 叹 啊(表示悲、喜、惊愕、怜悯等的感叹声)

3. **quite** [kwaɪt] 副 颇，相当地

4. **serious** [ˈsɪriəs] 形 严重的

5. **shot** [ʃɑt] 名 打针

6. **hurt** [hɜt] 动 疼痛 & 动 伤害

7. **soon** [sun] 副 不久，马上

8. **over** [ˈovɚ] 形 完毕的，结束的

9. **ouch** [autʃ] 叹 哎唷

10. **also** [ˈɔlso] 副 也，并且

11. **pill** [pɪl] 名 药丸

12. **time** [taɪm] 名 次，回

13. **after** [ˈæftɚ] 介 在……之后

14. **meal** [mil] 名 一餐

3 *Grammar Points* 语法重点 〰

会话 A

1. **Doctor, I think I have the flu**. 医生，我想我得了流行性感冒。

   a. 此处 think 之后省略了 that，亦即本句原为 "Doctor, I think that I have the flu."。本句亦可用 "Doctor, I'm afraid (that) I have the flu."（医生，恐怕我是得了流行性感冒。）来表示。本来自己是否得了流行性感冒，自己应该很清楚，但如果直接说 "Doctor, I have the flu." 则未免太过武断，对医生来说也不太尊重，故用 "I think (that)..." 或 "I'm afraid (that)..." 来缓和语气。

   例 It is going to rain today. 今天会下雨。

   比较

   I think (that) it is going to rain today. 我想今天会下雨。

   I'm afraid (that) it is going to rain today. 恐怕今天会下雨。

   b. have the flu 得了流行性感冒

   表 "得了流行性感冒"，flu 之前须置定冠词 the，而不可用不定冠词 a。

   例 John is not well because he has a flu. (×)

   → John is not well because he has the flu. (√)

   约翰因为得了流行性感冒，所以身体不舒服。

   have a cold 得了感冒

   = catch a cold

   = catch cold

   例 Put on your coat, or you will catch (a) cold.

   把外套穿起来，否则你会感冒。

2. **Do you have a cough, too?** 你也咳嗽吗？

   have a cough 咳嗽

   此处的 cough（咳嗽）是名词，但 cough 也可以作动词用。

   例 My father has a bad cough today. 我父亲今天咳得很厉害。

Cover your mouth when you cough. 咳嗽的时候要把嘴巴捂住。

3. **No. Not really.** 不，算不上真的咳嗽。

例 A: You swim a lot; you must enjoy swimming.

B: No. Not really. I swim for my health.

A: 你经常游泳，你一定很喜欢游泳。

B: 不，算不上真的喜欢。我是为了健康才游泳。

4. **Do you have a sore throat?** 喉咙会痛吗？

have a sore throat 喉咙痛

sore 是形容词，表"(疼)痛的"，指发炎或受伤的部位一碰就痛的感觉；此外，sore 还可用来表示肌肉方面"酸痛的"，如：have a sore arm(手臂酸痛)、have a sore leg(腿部酸痛)；ache [ek] 也可表"疼痛"，常常和其他词连用形成复合词，但 ache 则是指某部位持续疼痛的感觉，例如：

have a headache [ˈhɛdˌek] 头痛

have a toothache [ˈtuθˌek] 牙痛

have a stomachache [ˈstʌməkˌek] 胃痛

例 Don't talk too much when you have ┃a sore throat.
┃toothache.

喉咙 / 牙齿痛时，不要说太多话。

5. **A little. But I have a bit of a fever.** 一点点。但我有一点发烧。

= I have a little of a sore throat. But I have a bit of a fever.

a. a bit of... 有一点……

= a little bit of...

= a little of...

例 Let me give you a bit of advice. 让我来给你一点建议吧。

b. have a fever 发烧

例 The child is having a high fever. 这个小孩正在发高烧。

6. **Let me have a look.** 让我看看。

have a look at + 名词　看一看……

例 May I have a look at your picture? 我可以看一看你的照片吗？

注意

中文说"让我看看"，英文是"Let me have a look."。有许多学生为了俏皮常说成"Let me see see." 或"Let me look look."，固然有趣，但却是错误的用法，应该说"Let me have a look."才对。

会话 B

1. **It's quite serious. I think you need a shot.**

   情况相当严重，我想你得打一针。

   a. quite、fairly [ˈfɛrlɪ]、rather [ˈræðɚ]（相当地）、very（很）、extremely [ɪkˈstrimlɪ]（极，非常）等均为程度副词，在句中加强形容词或副词的词义。所谓副词是可修饰动词、形容词和副词的词类；所谓形容词则是可修饰名词和代词的词类。

      例 He studies hard. (hard 是副词，修饰动词 studies)
      他用功读书。

      She looks very beautiful. (very 是副词，修饰形容词 beautiful)
      她看起来很美。

      He studies very hard. (very 是副词，修饰副词 hard)
      他很用功读书。

      He is a young boy. (young 是形容词，修饰名词 boy)
      他是个年轻男孩。

      She is beautiful. (beautiful 是形容词，修饰代词 she)
      她很美。

   b. 在 a 项所列表示程度的副词中，依程度强弱排列如下：
      fairly（最弱），quite，rather，very，extremely（最强）

      例 It is fairly / quite / rather hot today.
      今天相当热。——但不是很热
      The car runs very fast. 这辆车跑起来很快。
      I feel extremely tired. 我觉得疲倦极了。

   c. shot 表"注射、打针"，是口语用法，正式的词为 injection [ɪnˈdʒɛkʃən]。
      give＋人＋a shot 给某人打针
      ＝ give＋人＋an injection
      get / take a shot（接受）打针

= get / take an injection

例 The nurse will give you a shot. 护士会替你打针。

Most children are afraid to take an injection.

大部分的小孩都害怕打针。

2. <u>Is it going to hurt?</u> 打针会不会痛呢？

a. 本句为 "It is going to hurt."变化而来的问句。

be going to + 动词　将会……

= will + 动词

例 It is going to rain this afternoon. 今天下午将会下雨。

= It will rain this afternoon.

I'm going to take a trip next week. 我下周将会去旅行。

= I will take a trip next week.

b. hurt 之后若无宾语时，译为 "疼痛"；有宾语时则译为 "伤害"。

例 My fingers hurt. 我的手指痛。

Nobody will hurt you. 没有人会伤害你。

3. **Don't worry. It'll soon be over.** 别担心。很快就会结束的。

"Don't worry."（别担心。）是会话中经常使用来安慰他人的话，同学宜记住。

worry [ˈwɜːɪ] 动 担心

worried [ˈwɜːɪd] 形 担心的

worry about... 担心……

= be worried about...

例 A: Oh, no. We'll miss the bus. We'll be late for school.

B: Don't worry. We can take a taxi.

A: 哦，糟了。我们会乘不上公交车，上学将会迟到。

B: 别担心。我们可以乘出租车。

We all worry about you very much.

= We are all worried about you very much.

我们都非常担心你。

4. **Ouch!** 哎唷！

"Ouch!"是英文中的拟声词，表因突来的疼痛而发出的叫声。其

229

他常见的拟声词尚有：Wow! [waʊ]（哇！）表示惊讶、赞叹，Uh-oh! [ˈʌˈo]（啊噢！）表示事情不妙，Uh-huh! [ˈʌˈhʌ]（嗯哼！）表示赞同之意。

例 A: Ouch! My stomach hurts. 哎唷！我的胃好痛。

　　B: You'd better go to a doctor. 你最好去看医生。

* stomach [ˈstʌmək] **名** 胃

　　A: Wow! What a beautiful girl! 哇！好漂亮的女孩！

　　B: Don't forget you are married. 别忘记你已经结婚了。

　　A: Johnny, stop drinking so much! 约翰尼，别喝那么多酒！

　　B: Uh-oh! There she goes again. 啊噢！她又来了。

　　A: How can we get the money we need? 我们要如何得到所需的钱？

　　B: We can borrow it from the bank. 我们可以向银行借。

　　A: Uh -huh! Let's do that. 嗯哼！就这么办。

5. **OK. It's done.** 好了，打完针了。

　= OK. It is done.

　= OK. It is finished.

　此处 done 是形容词，表"做完的"，等于 finished [ˈfɪnɪʃt]。

　　例 A: Have you finished your job? 你的工作做完了吗？

　　　　B: Yes, it's done already. 是的，已经做完了。

6. **Also, take these pills 3 times a day after meals.**
　还有，饭后服用这些药丸，一天三次。

　a. 表"吃药"的动词须用 take; 表"喝汤"的动词用 eat; 表"喝饮料、咖啡、牛奶等"时则动词用 drink。

　　例 I really hate taking medicine. 我实在很讨厌吃药。

　　　　Don't make noises when you eat soup. 喝汤时不要发出声音。

　　　　I drink a cup of coffee every day. 我每天喝一杯咖啡。

　b. 3 times a day 一天三次
　　表"次数"、"频率"的说法，中英文刚好相反，中文说"一天三次"，英文却说"三次一天"（3 times a day）。事实上，英文是把次数或频率放前面，之后再接时间。

例 Jack eats 4 meals a day. 杰克一天吃 4 餐。

They work 5 days a week. 他们一周工作 5 天。

The magazine is published once a month.

这本杂志一个月出版一次。

  * publish [ˈpʌblɪʃ] 动 出版（书籍、杂志等）

c. meal 是名词，指"一餐、一顿饭"的意思，有下列常见的用法：

例 She always has a small meal at lunch time.

她午餐时都吃的很少。

Don't read the newspaper at meals. 吃饭时不要看报纸。

My little sister likes to eat between meals. 我小妹喜欢吃零食。

4 ***Substitution*** 替换

1. Doctor, I think I have | the flu. 医生，我想我得了流行性感冒。
   | a cold. 医生，我想我得了感冒。

2. Do you have a | cough,
   | sore throat, | too?
   | fever,

你也咳嗽 / 喉咙痛 / 发烧吗？

3. It's | quite
   | very | serious.
   | extremely

情况相当 / 很 / 极为严重。

4. I think you need | a shot.   我想你得打一针。
   | an injection.

5. Is it going to | hurt? 会不会痛呢？
   | rain? 会不会下雨呢？

6. | Also, take these pills 3 times a day after meals.
   | Tom goes to Hong Kong once a week.
   | This magazine is published 4 times a month.

还有，饭后服用这些药丸，一天三次。

汤姆一个星期去香港一趟。

这本杂志一个月出版 4 次。

English Conversation on the Go

5　　　　　　*Exercises* 练习

I. Use the right word: 请选出适当的单词 :

quite	get	worried	done
have	the	a	eats

1. Peter isn't at work because he has _____ flu.

2. The noise is giving me _____ headache.

3. Tommy always makes noises when he _____ soup.

4. Can I _____ a look at your new watch?

5. It's _____ dangerous to drive when it's snowing.

6. If you _____ a shot, you'll get well very quickly.

7. I'm _____ about my father's health.

8. It's _____. I can stop working and go home now.

II. Complete the dialogue: 完成下列会话 :

A: Doctor, is it OK if I don't get a s_____?

B: Why? What are you w_____ about?

A: I think it will h_____.

B: It'll soon be o_____.

A: But can't I just t_____ some pills?

B: It will take q_____ a long time to get well.

A: It's alright.

B: Here. Take these pills three t_____ a day after meals.

A: Thanks, doctor.

Lesson 27

At the Zoo
在动物园

1 *Dialogue* 会话

会话 A

A: Can I take a picture with the lion, Dad?

B: Sure. But don't go too near the cage.

A: I'll stand behind the railing.

B: OK. Are you ready? Say "Cheese!"

A: Cheese!

B: That's a good one.

A: Lions are beautiful, aren't they?

B: They sure are. After all, the lion is "king of the beasts."

A: 我可以和狮子照张相吗，老爸？

B: 当然可以。不过不要太靠近笼子喔。

A: 我会站在栏杆后面。

B: 好了，准备好了吗？说"茄子"！

A: 茄子！

B: 这张照得很棒。

A: 狮子好漂亮喔，对不对？

B: 当然啦。毕竟，狮子是"万兽之王"啊！

会话 B

A: Wow! Look at that elephant. It's gigantic!

B: It sure is.

A: Can I feed it?

B: No. There's a no-feeding sign over there.

A: Poor elephant.

B: There aren't many elephants left in the world, are there?

A: People kill them for their tusks. Now they are an endangered species.

B: Man sometimes behaves worse than animals.

A: 哇！看那头大象，好大噢！

B: 它的确是。

A: 我可以喂它吗?

B: 不行。那儿有一个禁止喂食的标志。

A: 可怜的大象。

B: 世界上所剩的大象不多了，不是吗?

A: 人们为取得象牙而杀害它们，现在它们成了濒临绝种的动物。

B: 人类的行为有时候连禽兽都不如。

2 *Vocabulary & Idioms* 单词短语注解 ✍

会话 A

1. **zoo** [zu] 名 动物园

2. **picture** [ˈpɪktʃɚ] 名 相片, 照片

3. **lion** [ˈlaɪən] 名 狮子

4. **near** [nɪr] 介 靠近

5. **cage** [kedʒ] 名 笼子

6. **stand** [stænd] 动 站立

7. **behind** [bɪˈhaɪnd] 介 在……后面

8. **railing** [ˈrelɪŋ] 名 栏杆;围栏

9. **ready** [ˈrɛdɪ] 形 准备好的

10. **cheese** [tʃiz] 名 奶酪, 干酪

11. **after all** 毕竟, 终究

12. **king of the beasts** 万兽之王
    king [kɪŋ] 名 国王
    beast [bist] 名 野兽

会话 B

1. **elephant** [ˈɛləfənt] 名 象

2. **gigantic** [dʒaɪˈgæntɪk] 形 巨大的

3. **feed** [fid] 动 喂食

4. **no-feeding sign** 禁止喂食的标志
    sign [saɪn] 名 标志

5. **poor** [pʊr] 形 可怜的;贫穷的

6. **left** [lɛft] 形 剩下(来)的

7. **in the world** 在世界上
   world [wɜld] 名 世界

8. **kill** [kɪl] 动 杀(害)

9. **tusk** [tʌsk] 名 (象等的)长牙

10. **endangered** [ɪnˈdendʒəd] 形 濒临绝种的

11. **species** [ˈspiʃiz] 名 种，种类(单复数同形)

12. **man** [mæn] 名 人类(用单数形式);男人(复数形式为 men [mɛn])

13. **sometimes** [ˈsʌmˌtaɪmz] 副 有时候

14. **behave** [bɪˈhev] 动 行为，举止

15. **animal** [ˈænəml̩] 名 动物

3 *Grammar Points* 语法重点

会话 A

1. **Can I take a picture with the lion, Dad?**
   我可以和狮子照张相吗，老爸?
   take a picture with + 人 / 物　和某人 / 物拍照
   take a picture of + 人 / 物　拍某人 / 物的照片
   take a picture for + 人　替某人(做)拍照(的工作)
   例 May I take a picture with you? 我可以和你拍一张照片吗?
   I want to take a picture of these flowers.
   我要拍一张这些花的照片。
   Mister, can you take a picture for us?
   先生，可以请你为我们拍一张照片吗?

2. **But don't go too near the cage.** 不过不要太靠近笼子。
   = But don't go too close to the cage.
   a. 此处的 near 是介词，即等于 close to。
   例 His house is near the school. 他家离学校很近。
   = His house is close to the school.

b. cage 是"笼子"的意思，此处指关狮子的兽槛。

3. **I'll stand behind the railing.** 我会站在栏杆后面。

railing 是"栏杆"的意思，此处乃指防止游客靠近的狮笼的栏杆而言。

例 There is a man sitting on the railing. 有一名男子坐在栏杆上。

4. **Are you ready? Say "Cheese!"** 你准备好了吗？说"Cheese"！

a. ready 是形容词，表"准备好的"，有下列常见的用法：

be ready to + 动词原形　准备好要……

be ready for + 名词　为……准备妥当

例 Are you ready to go home? 你准备好要回家了吗？

　They are ready for the final exams. 他们已为期末考准备妥当。

b. cheese 本是"奶酪、干酪"之意，但是此处 Say "Cheese!" 可不要译成"说奶酪"。事实上这是照相时为取得笑容的用语，因为说 cheese 这个词时，嘴角向两旁拉开，看起来就像在笑一样，因此 Say "Cheese!" 真正的意思是要被照相的人微笑，就像我们照相时会说"来，笑一个"的意思是一样的。

5. **That's a good one.** 这张照得很棒。

"That's a good one." 是表示赞许的话，字面上的意思是"这个很不错。"通常在他人说了一句好话或一则好笑的笑话，我们可以说 "That's a good one." 以示嘉许之意；但依对话上下文判断，此处则是指被照相者（儿子或女儿）的微笑很甜，洗出来一定是一张很棒的照片。

6. **Lions are beautiful, aren't they?** 狮子好漂亮噢，对不对？

本句为标准的反意疑问句。其原则为：

叙述句为肯定时，接否定反意疑问句；

叙述句为否定时，接肯定反意疑问句。

此外，反意疑问句的主语一定为代词。

a. 叙述句有 be 动词，反意疑问句沿用 be 动词。

＊此处"Lions are beautiful, aren't they?"即属此种用法。

例 He is nice, isn't he? 他人很好，不是吗？

　You are not a student, are you? 你不是学生，不是吗？

b. 叙述句有助动词 will、can、have 等, 反意疑问句沿用该助动词。

例 She can dance, can't she? 她会跳舞,不是吗?

You haven't done it, have you? 你还没有做那件事,不是吗?

c. 叙述句只有动词, 反意疑问句则使用助动词 do、does。

例 He gets up early, doesn't he? 他很早起床,不是吗?

You like movies, don't you? 你喜欢电影,不是吗?

d. 叙述句为祈使句时, 反意疑问句一律用 will you。

例 Come over here, will you? 到这边来,好吗?

Stop smoking, will you? 不要再抽烟了,好吗?

e. 叙述句为 Let's... 开头, 反意疑问句一律用 shall we。

例 Let's go home, shall we? 咱们回家吧,好不好?

注意

Let 之后若接其他的人作宾语, 则反意疑问句要用 will you。

例 Let him go, will you? 放他走吧,好吗?

Let me do it, will you? 让我来做这件事,好吗?

7. **They sure are. After all, the lion is "king of the beasts."**

= They sure are beautiful. After all, the lion is "king of the beasts."

它们的确漂亮。毕竟,狮子是"万兽之王"啊。

a. 此处 sure 为副词, 表"的确",等于 surely。

b. After all, 主语 + 动词　毕竟,……

例 A: We can't give him too much work.

B: You're right. After all, he's just a new hand.

A: 我们不能给他太多工作。

B: 你说的对;毕竟,他只是个新手。

会话 B

1. **Wow! Look at that elephant. It's gigantic!**

哇! 看那头大象, 好大噢!

look at + 名词　看一看……

= take a look at + 名词

= have a look at + 名词

例 Look at that girl. Isn't she beautiful? 看那位女孩，是不是很漂亮啊？

= Take a look at that girl. Isn't she beautiful?

= Have a look at that girl. Isn't she beautiful?

2. **It sure is.** 它的确是很大。

= It sure is <u>gigantic</u>.

3. **Can I feed it?** 我可以喂它吗？

feed 是动词，表"喂食"的意思。

例 John feeds his dog every day. 约翰每天喂他的狗吃东西。

4. **Poor elephant.** 可怜的大象。

此处的 poor 是形容词，表示"可怜的"之意；但 poor 亦可表示"贫穷的"。

例 A: Mommy, Tom is pulling my hair.

B: Oh, poor girl. I'll tell him to stop.

A: 妈咪，汤姆拉我的头发。

B: 噢，可怜的孩子。我会叫他不要再这样了。

The poor man has no money to buy food.

那个贫穷的男子没有钱买食物。

5. **There aren't many elephants left in the world, are there?**

世界上所剩的大象不多了，不是吗？

此处的 left 是由动词 leave 演变而来的形容词，表示"剩下来的"，使用时置于名词之后。

例 I have no money left. 我没有剩下钱。

6. **People kill them for their tusks. Now they are an endangered species.**

人们为取得象牙而杀害它们，现在它们成了濒临绝种的动物。

a. tusk 是指象、海象、野猪等动物的"长牙"，是可数名词；而 ivory
[ˈaɪvərɪ] 则是指"象牙质料 / 材质"的意思。

例 An elephant has two tusks. 大象有两只象牙。

The pipe is made of ivory. 这个烟斗是象牙材质做的。

b. endangered species 濒临绝种的动植物

例 Tigers are one of the endangered species.

老虎是濒临绝种的动物之一。

注意

species 是单复数同形的名词，亦即可说 one species、two species、many species 等。本来英文中一般的名词由单数变成复数时，通常在字尾加 -s 或 -es，如：one book、two books 和 one inch（一英寸）、two inches；但有些名词的单数形式和复数形式拼法不变，此类单复数同形的名词，除了上述 species 之外，常见的尚有：fish（鱼）、sheep [ʃip]（绵羊）、deer [dɪr]（鹿）、salmon [ˈsæmən]（鲑鱼）、buffalo [ˈbʌfəˌlo]（水牛）、antelope [ˈæntəlop]（羚羊）等。这些词的确令人困扰，但幸好它们为数并不多，只要见一个记一个，日子一久功力加深，问题自可迎刃而解。

7. **Man sometimes behaves worse than animals.**

人类的行为有时候连禽兽都不如。

a. behave 是动词，表"行为、举止"的意思，有下列常见用法：

behave oneself 循规蹈矩，守规矩

behave well 行为表现良好

例 Behave yourself, or you will be punished.

规矩一点，否则你会被处罚

Tom behaves well in school. 汤姆在校行为表现良好。

b. worse [wɝs] 副 更坏地（是副词 badly 的比较级）

worst [wɝst] 副 最坏地（是副词 badly 的最高级）

better [ˈbɛtɚ] 副 较好地（是副词 well 的比较级）

best [bɛst] 副 最好地（是副词 well 的最高级）

例 She dances badly.

她舞跳得很糟。

I dance worse than she.

我舞跳得比她更糟。

Peter dances worst of the three boys.

三个男孩中彼得舞跳得最糟。

She sings well.

她唱歌很好听。

I sing better than she.

我唱歌比她好听。

Mary sings best of the three girls.

三个女孩中玛丽歌唱得最好。

4   *Substitution* 替换

1. Can I take a picture with the lion, Dad?
   Can I take a picture of the monkey, Mom?
   Excuse me. Can you take a picture for us?

   我可以和狮子照张相吗，爸爸？

   我可以给猴子照张相吗，妈妈？

   打扰一下，可以请你为我们照张相吗？

2. Are you ready? 你准备好了吗？
   Are you ready to go? 你准备好要走了吗？
   Are you ready for lunch? 你准备好吃午餐了吗？

3. Lions are beautiful, aren't they? 狮子好漂亮喔，对不对？
   Bill can't speak Japanese, can he? 比尔不会说日文，是吗？
   May goes to bed late, doesn't she? 梅很晚睡，对不对？
   Stop talking, will you? 别讲话了，好吗？
   Let's take a break, shall we? 咱们休息一下吧，好不好？

4. Look
   Take a look ｜at that elephant. 看那头大象。
   Have a look

5 Exercises 练习

I. Use the right word: 请选出适当的单词：

worse	will	don't	shall
ready	isn't	take	can't

1. Are you _____? We're all set to leave.
2. Jane's coming to the party, _____ she?
3. Tom can speak English, _____ he?
4. Thomas and James work for you, _____ they?
5. Let's go home now, _____ we?
6. Leave him alone, _____ you?
7. She sings _____ than her sister.
8. Peter likes to _____ pictures of people.

II. Complete the dialogue: 完成下列会话：

A: Are lions an endangered s_____, Dad?
B: They s_____ are.
A: How come? They're "king of the beasts," a_____ they?
B: Yes. But people kill them for their hide ([haɪd] 兽皮).
A: That's bad. P_____ lions.
B: Sometimes man really b_____ worse than animals.
A: They sure do. Let's go home, s_____ we? I don't feel well suddenly.
B: OK. I'm r_____. Let's go.

Lesson 28

Going to the Movies
看电影

会话 A

A: Can I have two tickets for *Titanic*, please?

B: For what time?

A: The 9:30 p.m. show, please.

B: I'm afraid it's full. How about the midnight show?

A: That'll be fine. Can I have our seats up front, please?

B: Sure. That'll be twenty dollars, please.

A: 可以给我两张《泰坦尼克号》的票吗?

B: 什么时间的?

A: 麻烦晚上 9 点半那一场。

B: 恐怕已经客满了，午夜场如何？

A: 可以，请给我前排的座位好吗？

B: 没问题。麻烦你总共是 20 美元。

会话 B

A: Where were you last night?

B: I was at the movies. I went to see *Titanic*.

A: How was it?

B: It was fantastic. The main actor and actress really did a good job.

A: Sounds like it was a very good movie.

B: You can say that again!

A: 你昨晚到哪儿去了？

B: 我在看电影，我跑去看《泰坦尼克号》。

A: 好看吗？

B: 非常好看。男女主角演得真是棒极了。

A: 听你这么说好像是部很棒的电影。

B: 你说的一点也没错。

2 *Vocabulary & Idioms* 单词短语注解

会话 A

1. **Titanic** [taɪˈtænɪk]名 泰坦尼克号（电影名）
   the Titanic 泰坦尼克号轮船（英国巨轮，1912 年在其处女航中于纽芬兰南方海面撞上冰山而沉没）

2. **show** [ʃo]名（电影、电视、戏剧、广播的）演出节目

3. **full** [fʊl]形 满的

4. **midnight show** 午夜场

会话 B

1. **were** [wɜ] be 动词 are 的过去式

2. **was** [wɑz] be 动词 am、is 的过去式

3. **went** [wɛnt] 动词 go 的过去式

4. **fantastic** [fænˈtæstɪk]形 很棒的，极好的

5. **main** [men]形 主要的，最重要的

6. **actor** [ˈæktə]名 男演员

7. **actress** [ˈæktrɪs]名 女演员

8. **did** [dɪd] 动词 do 的过去式

3 *Grammar Points* 语法重点

标题

go to the movies 看电影
movie [ˈmuvɪ]名 电影
go to the movies 表"看电影"，movies 须用复数。但表"看一场电影"则可有下列用法：
watch a movie 看一场电影

= see a movie

= take in a movie

例 He seldom goes to the movies. 他很少看电影。

We are going to <u>watch</u> a movie tonight.

= We are going to <u>see</u> a movie tonight.

= We are going to <u>take in</u> a movie tonight.

我们今晚要去看一场电影。

会话 A

1. **Can I have two tickets for _Titanic_, please?**

可以给我两张《泰坦尼克号》的票吗？

ticket [ˈtɪkɪt] 名 票，入场券

例 Molly has two free tickets for the concert.

茉莉有两张免费的演唱会门票。

* free [fri] 形 免费的

2. **For what time?** 什么时间的？ / 你要什么时间的票？

= For what time would you like the tickets?

此处 "For what time?" 是由 "For what time would you like the tickets?" 简化而来。

3. **The 9:30 p.m. show, please.**

= I'd like to have tickets for the 9:30 p.m. show，please.

麻烦晚上 9:30 那一场。/ 麻烦我要晚 9:30 那一场的票。

show 本来是指表演、演出，此处则是指电影。

例 We will go to see the 3:00 p.m. show (of the movie).

= We will go to see the movie that is shown at 3:00 p.m.

我们将去看下午 3 点放映的那场电影。

4. **I'm afraid it's full. How about the midnight show?**

= I'm afraid that the tickets are sold out. What about the midnight show?

恐怕已经客满了 / 恐怕票已经卖光了，午夜场如何？

a. full 表示 "满的" 之意，有下列常见用法：

be full of... 充满……

例 The house is full of people. 房子里挤满了人。

b. be sold out 卖完，卖光

例 The tickets for the movie have been sold out.

这场电影的票已经卖光了。

c. How about + 名词 / 动名词？ ……如何？

= What about + 名词 / 动名词？

例 A: How | about another piece of pizza? 再来一块比萨饼如何？
　　　 What|

B: No, thanks. I have had enough. 不，谢了。我已经吃饱了。

How about going to the movies tonight? 今晚去看电影如何？

= What about going to the movies tonight?

5. **Can I have our seats up front, please?** 请给我前排的座位好吗？

Can I have a seat..., please? 请给我……的座位好吗？

例 Can I have a seat in the back, please? 请给我后面的座位好吗？

Can I have a seat near / by the aisle, please?

请给我靠走道的座位好吗？

Can I have a seat towards the center, please?

请给我靠中间的座位好吗？

Can I have a seat on the left / right side, please?

请给我左 / 右边的座位好吗？

6. **That'll be twenty dollars, please.** 麻烦你总共是 20 美元。

That'll be + 金钱　一共是……（钱）

= That'll be + 金钱 + in total

= All this comes to + 金钱

例 A: How much do I owe you? 我要付你多少钱？

B: That'll be 50 dollars. 一共是 50 美元。

= That'll be 50 dollars in total.

= All this comes to 50 dollars.

7. 其他和电影有关的用语如下：

例 When will the new | movie | be on? 这部新片何时上映？
　　　　　　　　　　　 film

* film [fɪlm] 名 电影，影片

Let me treat you to a movie, OK? 让我请你去看电影，要不要？

Is *Titanic* showing yet?《泰坦尼克号》上映了吗？

That movie is a rerun; that's why it's cheaper.

那部电影是回放，所以比较便宜。

* rerun [ˈriˌrʌn] 名 回放的影片 / 节目

会话 B

1. **Where were you last night?** 你昨晚到哪儿去了？

此处的 were 是 be 动词 are 的过去式。

注意

过去时是表示在过去时间所发生的事，中英文在表示过去时时态时差别很大。中文里会用过去时间来表示，动词维持不变，英文虽也用过去时间，但动词形态会改变。例如中文说："我爱她。"和"我 3 年前很爱她。"动词"爱"不改变，但英文说："I love her."和"I loved her three years ago.",动词由现在时 love 变成过去时 loved。因此我们必须随时注意，以免犯下语法错误。

a. 不规则变化的 be 动词：

时态 人称	现在时	过去时
第一人称单数	I am...	I was...
第一人称复数	We are...	We were...
第二人称单数	You are...	You were...
第二人称复数	You are...	You were...
第三人称单数	He/She/It is...	He/She/It was...
第三人称复数	They are...	They were...

b. 一般动词的过去时分为规则和不规则变化：

（1）规则变化——动词原形加-ed 或-d，或去 y 加-ied，如下列：

现在时　　　　　　　　过去时

want [wɑnt] 　　→　　wanted [ˈwɑntɪd] （要）

look [lʊk] 　　→　　looked [lʊkt] （看）

play [ple] 　　→　　played [pled] （玩）

like [laɪk]	→	liked [laɪkt]	（喜欢）
hate [het]	→	hated [ˈhetɪd]	（讨厌）
study [ˈstʌdɪ]	→	studied [ˈstʌdɪd]	（读书）

（2）不规则变化——见一个记一个

现在时		过去时	
go [go]	→	went [wɛnt]	（走）
do [du]	→	did [dɪd]	（做）
see [si]	→	saw [sɔ]	（看）
feel [fil]	→	felt [fɛlt]	（感觉）
think [θɪŋk]	→	thought [θɔt]	（想）
buy [baɪ]	→	bought [bɔt]	（买）
teach [titʃ]	→	taught [tɔt]	（教）
catch [kætʃ]	→	caught [kɔt]	（捉）
hold [hold]	→	held [hɛld]	（握）
rise [raɪz]	→	rose [roz]	（升起）
sing [sɪŋ]	→	sang [sæŋ]	（唱歌）
ride [raɪd]	→	rode [rod]	（骑）
drive [draɪv]	→	drove [drov]	（开、驾驶）
write [raɪt]	→	wrote [rot]	（写）
tell [tɛl]	→	told [told]	（告诉）
speak [spik]	→	spoke [spok]	（说）
take [tek]	→	took [tʊk]	（拿）
have [hæv]	→	had [hæd]	（有）
sell [sɛl]	→	sold [sold]	（卖）

c. 过去时使用的时机：

过去时是表过去所发生的事、动作或状态，通常和过去时间连用。

例 I go to school every day. (现在时) 我每天去上学。

I went to school yesterday. (过去时) 我昨天去上学。

d. 故本篇会话第一句 "Where were you last night?" 由于句尾的 last night (昨晚) 是过去的时间，因此 be 动词不能用现在时

are，而须用过去时 were。

2. **I was at the movies.** 我在看电影。

be at the movies 在看电影

例 They are probably at the movies now. 他们现在很可能在看电影。

3. **It was fantastic.** 它很棒。

= It was great.

= It was wonderful.

例 A: How was the party last night?

B: It was fantastic; everyone had a great time.

A: 昨晚的派对如何？

B: 棒极了，每个人都玩得很开心。

4. **The main actor and actress really did a good job.**

男女主角演得真是棒极了。

a. main actor 男主角

= lead actor [ˌlidˈæktɚ]

main actress 女主角

= lead actress [ˌlidˈæktrɪs]

例 Harrison Ford is the main actor in the movie.

哈里森·福特是这部电影的男主角。

b. do a good job 表现优异，做得很好

= do (very) well

例 He did a good job in the speech contest.

= He did very well in the speech contest.

他在演讲比赛中表现优异。

* contest [ˈkɑntɛst] 名 比赛，竞赛

5. **Sounds like it was a very good movie.**

听起来好像是部很棒的电影。

Sounds like + 主语 + 动词 听起来好像……

本句型原由 "It sounds like + 主语 + 动词" 省略而来。

例 A: What do you think of the singer's voice?

B: Not very good. Sounds like he has a cold.

A: 你觉得这位歌手的声音如何？

B: 不太好,听起来好像他感冒了。

注意

就语法而言, "sound like..." 之中的 like 为介词, 之后只能接名词作宾语, 不能接主语和动词; 若要接主语和动词, 则须改用 "sound as if..." (听起来仿佛……),因为 as if 才是连词。但在现代英文中,已把 like 视为介词, 之后接名词作宾语, 又视为连词, 之后接主语和动词。

例 It sounds like a good idea. 这听起来像是个好主意。

He sounds <u>as if</u> he knows everything about it.

= He sounds <u>like</u> he knows everything about it.
听他的口气仿佛他对这件事知道得一清二楚。

6. **You can say that again!** 你说的一点也没错!

本句为赞同他人意见的用语,为极口语的用法。

例 A: Mary is very beautiful. 玛丽漂亮极了。

B: You can say that again! 你说的一点也没错!

---

4   *Substitution* 替换   ♋

1. We are going to $\begin{vmatrix} \text{watch} \\ \text{see} \\ \text{take in} \end{vmatrix}$ a movie tonight.

我们今晚要去看一场电影。

2. I'm afraid (that) $\begin{vmatrix} \text{it's full.} \\ \text{the tickets are sold out.} \end{vmatrix}$

恐怕已经客满了 / 票已经卖光了。

3. Can I have a seat $\begin{vmatrix} \text{up front,} \\ \text{in the back,} \\ \text{by the aisle,} \\ \text{towards the center,} \\ \text{on the left side,} \end{vmatrix}$ please?

请给我前排 / 后面 / 靠走道 / 靠中间 / 左边的座位好吗?

4. That'll be twenty dollars, please.
   That'll be twenty dollars in total, please.
   All this comes to twenty dollars, please.
   麻烦你总共是 20 美元。

5. Where | were you / were they / was she | last night? 你 / 他们 / 她昨晚到哪儿去了？

6. It was | fantastic. / great. / wonderful. | 它很棒。

5 Exercises 练习

I. Use the right word: 请选出适当的单词：

| if | did | caught | like |
| take | out | back | full |

1. I'm bored. Let's go _____ in a movie tonight.
2. The seven o'clock show is sold _____, I'm afraid.
3. When I go to the movies, I like to sit in the _____.
4. The room is _____ of noisy kids.
5. Jack _____ very well on the test.
6. Wendy sings as _____ she has something in her throat.
7. Sounds _____ nobody is interested in going to the park.
8. I _____ a cold last week and I'm still feeling bad.

II. Complete the dialogue: 完成下列会话：

A: Where's Sue? I thought she was g_____ to the movies with me.

B: She was a_____ the movies.

A: Whom did she go with?

B: She w_____ with Uncle John.

A: Which movie did they go to s_____?

B: I think Uncle John t_____ her to see *A bug's Life*.

A: That's a great movie.

B: You can s_____ that again!

A: Let's go see the ten o'clock s_____.

B: Sure. Why not?

Lesson 29

Job Interviews
求职面试

1 *Dialogue* 会话   📖

会话 A

A: Tell me, Mr. Wang. Why do you want to join our company?

B: It has a good reputation.

A: Do you have any work experience?

B: Not much. But I am willing to learn.

A: Why did you quit your last job?

B: I think I'll have a better future with your company.

A: 告诉我，王先生。为何你想加入我们公司？

B: 贵公司有良好的声誉。

A: 你有什么工作经验吗？

B: 不太多。但我很愿意学习。

A: 你为什么辞去上一个工作?

B: 我认为在贵公司我会比较有前途。

会话 B

A: Do you have any questions?

B: Yes. Will I have to work overtime?

A: Sometimes.

B: How about holidays?

A: After a year, you'll get an annual leave of seven days.

B: And is there a year-end bonus?

A: That depends. If you work hard and the company makes money, you'll get one.

B: That sounds fair.

A: 你有什么问题吗?

B: 有。我必须要加班吗?

A: 有时候要。

B: 那么假期呢?

A: 满 1 年后，你每年就会有 7 天的假期。

B: 是否有年终奖金呢?

A: 那要视情况而定。如果你工作努力而且公司赚钱的话就会有。

B: 听起来很合理。

2 Vocabulary & Idioms 单词短语注解

会话 A

1. **interview** [ˈɪntəˌvju] 名 面谈；会晤
2. **join** [dʒɔɪn] 动 加入，参加
3. **company** [ˈkʌmpənɪ] 名 公司
4. **reputation** [ˌrɛpjəˈteʃən] 名 名声，声誉
5. **experience** [ɪkˈspɪrɪəns] 名 经验
6. **willing** [ˈwɪlɪŋ] 形 愿意的
7. **learn** [lɜn] 动 学习
8. **did** [dɪd] 是助动词 do 的过去式
9. **quit** [kwɪt] 动 辞 (职)
10. **future** [ˈfjutʃə] 名 未来，将来

会话 B

1. **question** [ˈkwɛstʃən] 名 问题
2. **overtime** [ˈovəˌtaɪm] 副 超出时间地
3. **holiday** [ˈhɑləˌde] 名 假日，休假
4. **annual** [ˈænjuəl] 形 每年的；一年一次的
5. **leave** [liv] 名 准假，休假 (期间)
6. **year-end** [ˈjɪrˌɛnd] 形 年底的，年终的
7. **bonus** [ˈbonəs] 名 奖金；分红
8. **depend** [dɪˈpɛnd] 动 视……而定
9. **hard** [hɑrd] 副 努力地
10. **make money** 赚钱
11. **fair** [fɛr] 形 公平的，合理的

3 **Grammar Points** 语法重点 〰

会话 A

1. **Why do you want to join our company?**
    为何你想加入我们公司？

    a. Why do you want to + 动词？ 为何你想 / 要……？

        例 Why do you want to learn English? 为何你想学英语呢？

    b. join 是动词，表示"加入、参加"的意思，有下列常见的用法：
        join + 人 + 动名词 加入某人做……

        例 Let's join them in singing the song. 咱们加入他们唱歌的行列吧。

2. **It has a good reputation.** 贵公司有良好的声誉。
    此处 It 指上一句的 company。

3. **Do you have any work experience?** 你有任何工作经验吗？
    work experience 工作经验

    例 He has a lot of work experience. 他有很多的工作经验。

4. **But I am willing to learn.** 但我很愿意学习。
    be willing to + 动词 愿意（做）……
    be unwilling to + 动词 不愿意（做）……

    *   unwilling [ʌnˈwɪlɪŋ] 形 不愿意的

        例 She is willing to help the poor. 她愿意去帮助穷人。

        He is unwilling to work in his father's company.
        他不愿意在父亲的公司做事。

5. **Why did you quit your last job?** 你为什么辞去上一个工作？
    = Why did you <u>resign from</u> your last job?

    注意

    quit 和 resign [rɪˈzaɪn] 均可表"辞（职）"，但 quit 直接加宾语 job，
    resign 则须先置 from 再接宾语 job。此外，quit 亦可表"戒除、放弃"
    之意，此时可等于 give up。

    例 Carlos will never quit his job. 卡洛斯绝不会辞去他的工作。

    = Carlos will never resign from his job.

My doctor told me to quit smoking. 我的医生叫我戒烟。

= My doctor told me to give up smoking.

6. **I think I'll have a better future with your company.**

我认为在贵公司我会比较有前途。

future 是名词，表示"未 / 将来"，有下列常见的用法：

carve out a bright future 开创光明的前途

* carve [kɑrv] 动 开创(命运、事业等)

* bright [braɪt] 形 光明的

例 You should carve out a bright future by working hard.

你应该努力工作开创光明的前途。

会话 B

1. **Will I have to work overtime?** 我必须要加班吗？

work overtime 加班

例 They're working overtime to finish the job on time.

他们正在加班以便准时完成这项工作。

2. **sometimes** [ˈsʌmˌtaɪmz] 副 有时候

= on occasion [əˈkeʒən]

= occasionally [əˈkeʒənlɪ]

= every now and then

例 He sometimes visits me. 他有时候会来看我。

= He visits me on occasion.

= He visits me occasionally.

= He visits me every now and then.

3. **After a year, you'll get an annual leave of seven days.**

满 1 年后,你每年就会有 7 天的假期。

此处的 leave 是名词，表"休假、假期"的意思。

ask for leave 请假

例 The workers seldom ask for leave. 那些员工很少请假。

be on leave 休假中

be on holiday 度假中

= be on vacation [veˈkeʃən]

注意

be on leave 指一般的休假而言，时间较短约一天或两天；be on holiday / vacation 则指时间较长的度假，有时可达一个月之久。

例 The soldiers are on leave. 那些士兵正在休假中。

They are on holiday in Hawaii. 他们正在夏威夷度假。

= They are on vacation in Hawaii.

4. **And is there a year-end bonus?** 是否有年终奖金呢？

year-end bonus 年终奖金

例 The workers will get a year-end bonus this year.

员工们今年将领到年终奖金。

5. **That depends.** 那要视情况而定。

= It depends.

例 A: Will you buy me a bicycle, Dad?

B: That / It depends. If you do well on the exam, yes.

A: 老爸，你会买自行车给我吗？

B: 那要看情形而定。如果你考试考得好就会买给你。

6. **If you work hard and the company makes money, you'll get one.**

如果你工作努力而且公司赚钱的话就会有。

表示"赚钱"的动词除了 make 以外，还可以用 earn [ɜn]。

make money 赚钱

= earn money

make a fortune 赚大钱

= earn a fortune

= make/earn a lot of money

make a living by... 靠……维生

= earn a living by...

例 Eric made a fortune in the stock market.

= Eric earned a fortune in the stock market.

= Eric made / earned a lot of money in the stock market.

艾力克在股票市场赚了一大笔钱。

He makes a living by driving a taxi. 他靠开出租车维生。

= He earns a living by driving a taxi.

7. **That sounds fair.** 听起来很合理。

此处 sound 为感官动词，表"听起来"。感官动词计有：look（看起来）、sound（听起来）、taste（尝起来）、smell（闻起来）、feel（感觉起来），之后接形容词或"like + 名词"。

例 The little boy looks shy. 那小男孩看起来很害羞。

* shy [ʃaɪ] 形 害羞的

The music sounds beautiful. 这音乐听起来很美。

The medicine tastes sweet. 这药尝起来甜甜的。

The perfume smells like flowers. 这香水闻起来像花的味道。

Her hair feels like silk. 她的头发摸起来像丝一样。

4 **_Substitution_ 替换**

1. Why do you want to join our company? 为何你想加入我们公司？
   wear long hair? 为何你想留长发呢？

2. But I am willing to learn. 但我很愿意学习。
   Helen is unwilling to work overtime. 海伦不愿意加班。

3. The doctor told my father to quit / give up drinking.

   医生叫我爸爸戒酒。

4. That / It depends. 那要视情况而定。

5. Carlos makes / earns a living by teaching. / writing novels.

   卡洛斯靠教书／写小说维生。

6. That sounds fair. 听起来很合理。
   You look terrible. 你看起来糟透了。
   The steak tastes good. 这牛排吃起来很棒。
   The milk smells sour. 这牛奶闻起来酸酸的。
   I'm feeling better today. 我今天觉得好多了。

5 **Exercises** 练习 ☪

I. Use the right word: 请选出适当的单词 :

on	quit	like	future
fortune	occasion	annual	give

1. If you're not happy with your job, just _____.

2. The doctor told me to _____ up drinking.

3. The smart young man has a bright _____.

4. Mr. Li takes his family on a trip on _____.

5. Mr. Black isn't in the office today. He's _____ leave.

6. Mr. Chen makes a _____ by selling houses.

7. This chicken tastes _____ fish.

8. You should go for an _____ check-up.

   * check-up ['tʃɛkˌʌp] 名 健康检查

II. Complete the dialogue: 完成下列会话 :

A: Do you have any e_____ in teaching English?

B: No. But I'm w_____ to work hard.

A: That's good. So you won't mind working o_____, will you?

B: No, not at all. But I won't have to work during the summer v_____, will I?

A: It d_____. If you like, you can teach summer classes.

B: How much can I make if I do?

A: Not much.

B: That doesn't s_____ very good.

A: I thought you said you're willing to work hard!

Lesson 30

Emergency Calls
紧急电话

1 *Dialogue* 会话

会话 A

A: This is an emergency call! Get an ambulance here right away.

B: Where are you calling from?

A: I'm at No.10 Zhong Hua Road.

B: What's the problem?

A: A taxi ran into a truck.

A: 这是紧急电话！请马上派一部救护车来这里。

B: 你从哪里打的电话？

A: 我在中华路 10 号。

B: 发生了什么事？

A: 一辆出租车撞上了一部卡车。

会话 B

A: Fire! There's a fire. Come quick!

B: Where's the fire?

A: At No.7 Kaifeng Street.

B: What's burning?

A: My restaurant is on fire.

B: How did it happen?

A: A gas tank exploded.

B: We'll be right there!

A: 失火了！发生火灾了，快点来。

B: 哪里发生火灾了？

A: 在开封街 7 号。

B: 什么东西着火了？

A: 我的餐馆烧起来了。

B: 怎么发生的？

A: 煤气罐爆炸。

B: 我们马上到！

② **Vocabulary & Idioms** 单词短语注解

会话 A

1. **emergency** [ɪˋmɝdʒənsɪ] 形 紧急的

2. **ambulance** [ˋæmbjələns] 名 救护车

3. **ran** [ræn] 是动词 run [rʌn]（跑）的过去式

4. **truck** [trʌk] 名 卡车，货车

会话 B

1. **fire** [faɪr] 名 火（不可数）；火灾（可数）

2. **quick** [kwɪk] 副 快速地，迅速地

3. **burn** [bɝn] 动 燃烧（burning [ˋbɝnɪŋ] 是 burn 的现在分词）

4. **happen** [ˋhæpən] 动 发生

5. **gas tank** [ˋgæsˌtæŋk] 名 煤气罐
   gas [gæs] 名 煤气
   tank [tæŋk] 名（水、油、煤气等的）罐，槽

6. **explode** [ɪkˋsplod] 动 爆炸（exploded [ɪkˋsplodɪd] 是 explode 的过去式）
   Be careful! The bomb will explode at any moment.
   小心！这颗炸弹随时都会爆炸。
   * bomb [bɑm] 名 炸弹

③ **Grammar Points** 语法重点 〰

会话 A

1. **This is an emergency call!** 这是紧急电话！
   此处的 emergency 是形容词，表"紧急的"之意；但 emergency 也可作名词，表"紧急（情况）"。
   例 This KTV has no emergency exits. 这家 KTV 没有紧急出口。

* exit [ˈɛgzɪt] 名 出口，安全门

A: What should you do in case of an emergency?

B: Call 911.

A: 万一发生紧急情况时你该怎么办?

B: 打电话给 911。

* 国内的紧急电话号码是 119, 在美国则是 911。

2. **Get an ambulance here right away.**

请马上派一部救护车来这里。

a. 本句为祈使句。所谓祈使句就是以动词原形开头的句子。

例 <u>You should</u> put on your coat. (一般句) 你应该把外套穿起来。

→ Put on your coat. (祈使句) 把外套穿起来。

You should be quiet. (一般句) 你应该要安静。

→ Be quiet! (祈使句) 安静!

<u>You should</u> keep away from that dog. (一般句)
你应该不要靠近那只狗。

→ Keep away from that dog! (祈使句) 不要靠近那只狗。

b. right away 立刻, 马上

= immediately [ɪˈmidɪɪtlɪ] 副

= instantly [ˈɪnstəntlɪ] 副

例 The police came to help me <u>right away</u>. 警察立刻赶来援助我。

= The police came to help me <u>immediately</u>.

= The police came to help me <u>instantly</u>.

3. **I'm at No.10 Zhong Hua Road.** 我在中华路 10 号。

通常与门牌号连用时, 应使用介词 at; 与街道连用时, 则与介词 on
连用。

a. at + 门牌号码　在几号

例　I live <u>at</u> No.10 Zhong Hua Road. 我住在中华路 10 号。

但 : I live <u>on</u> Zhong Hua Road. 我住在中华路上。

b. at +(表年龄的)数字　在几岁时

= at the age of + 数字

例 He got married <u>at 27</u>. 他在 27 岁时结婚。

= He got married at the age of 27.

   c. at the speed of + 数字　以……速度

例 The bus was going at the speed of 60 miles per hour.
那辆公交车当时正以每小时 60 英里的速度前进。

4. **What's the problem?** 发生了什么事？

= What's the matter?

= What's wrong?

例 A: You look sad. What's the problem?
B: My girlfriend left me.
A: 看你愁容满面的，发生了什么事？
B: 我的女友离开我了。

5. **A taxi ran into a truck.** 一辆出租车撞上了一部卡车。

= A taxi hit a truck.

run into... 撞到……

= hit [hɪt] 动 碰撞（过去式亦为 hit）

例 The car ran into the tree at a high speed. 那辆车以高速撞上那棵树。
= The car hit the tree at a high speed.

注意

run into + 人　和某人不期而遇

= bump into + 人

* bump [bʌmp] 动 撞击

例 I ran into an old friend on my way here.
= I bumped into an old friend on my way here.
在我来这里的途中，我和一位老朋友不期而遇。

会话 B

1. **Fire! There's a fire.** 失火了！发生火灾了。

   a. fire 表"火"时，是不可数名词；表"火灾"时，则为可数名词，
可说 a fire, two fires...。

例 Little Billy is afraid of fire. 小比利怕火。

A fire broke out in the downtown area yesterday.

昨天在市区发生了一起火灾。

b. 有关 fire 的重要用法如下 :

be on fire 着火 ; 燃烧中

set fire to + 名词　放火烧……

= set + 名词 + on fire

* set 的过去式亦为 set。

例 The house is on fire! 那幢房子着火了!

Someone set fire to <u>the building</u>. 有人放火烧了那栋楼。

= Someone set <u>the building</u> on fire.

2. **Come quick!** 快点来!

= Come quickly!

注意

quick 原为形容词, 表"快 / 迅速的", 但在口语中, quick 也可作副词用, 等于 quickly [ˈkwɪklɪ], 由于 quick 比 quickly 说起来较简洁, 故在口语中常用 quick 代替 quickly。

例 David is a <u>quick</u> walker. (形容词) 大卫走路很快。

Come <u>quick</u>; something terrible has happened. (副词)

快来呀, 发生可怕的事情啦。

3. **What's burning?** 什么东西在燃烧 / 着火了?

此处的 burning 是动词 burn(燃烧)的现在分词。

be 动词 + 现在分词　正在……

例 The whole building is burning. 整栋建筑都烧起来了。

The bad guys burned the house to the ground.

那些坏蛋把房子烧为平地。

4. **We'll be right there!** 我们马上到!

= We'll be there <u>right away</u>!

= We'll be there <u>immediately</u>!

此处的 right 是副词, 作强调用法。

4

Substitution 替换

1. Get an ambulance here | right away. | immediately. | instantly.

请马上派一部救护车来这里。

2. He graduated from college | at 15. | at the age of 15.

他 15 岁时就大学毕业了。

3. What's | the problem? | the matter? | wrong?   发生了什么事？／怎么了？

4. A taxi | ran into | hit | a truck. 一辆出租车撞上了一部卡车。

5. I | ran into | bumped into | one of my high school classmates last night.

我昨晚和一位高中同学不期而遇。

6. Come | quick! | quickly!   快点来！

7. The crazy man | set fire to his own house. | set his own house on fire.

那个疯子放火烧了自己的房子。

5

Exercises 练习

I. Use the right word: 请选出适当的单词：

burned	fire	Be	ran
emergency	on	away	into

1. In case of an _____, calmly leave through that door.

2. Please come right _____, doctor. My mother is very sick.

3. My friend's restaurant is _____ Sesame Street.

4. I bumped _____ my teacher in the library.

5. Jenny _____ into a glass door and broke her glasses.

6. The little shop was _____ to the ground.

7. A _____ broke out on the seventh floor.

8. _____ quiet, please. I can't hear the student's answer.

II. Complete the dialogue: 完成下列会话 :

A: Police! Come q_____.

B: Why? What's the m_____?

A: I think someone is robbing the bank.

B: Where are you c_____ from?

A: I'm o_____ Hoping East Road. Come right away.

B: We'll be r_____ there.

Answers
参考答案

Lesson 1

I. 1. See   2. going   3. What's   4. Not
    5. Good   6. How   7. much   8. Same

II. Not, bad, fine, Take, care

Lesson 2

I. 1. Excuse   2. but   3. beg   4. mention
    5. all   6. meet   7. problem   8. Where

II. Excuse, me, not, but, she, lot, welcome

Lesson 3

I. 1. How   2. What's   3. old   4. Where
    5. May   6. does   7. will   8. come

II. your, are, How, come, American, pardon

Lesson 4

I. 1. meet   2. This   3. to   4. It's
    5. call   6. family   7. Who's   8. These

II. going, bad, Who's, This, my, Glad, pleased

Lesson 5

I. 1. do   2. works   3. for(或 in)   4. like
    5. job   6. What   7. How   8. Same

II. this, do, do, And, How, too

Lesson 6

I. 1. it   2. half   3. next   4. time
    5. quarter   6. watch   7. o   8. midnight

II. by, noon, late, time, see, mean, fast, to

Lesson 7
I.   1. day   2. today's   3. girls'   4. it
      5. today   6. your   7. sixth   8. our

II.   date, It's, Why, Because, the

Lesson 8
I.   1. having   2. like   3. are   4. has
      5. It's   6. have   7. is   8. doing

II.   hot, summer, rain, rainy, cool, see, raining

Lesson 9
I.   1. Will   2. May   3. This   4. take
      5. out   6. Few   7. a   8. as

II.   there, moment, message, calling, This, Hold, ahead, ask

Lesson 10
I.   1. this   2. do   3. place   4. would
      5. with   6. to   7. code   8. service

II.   May, make, name, all, right, like, fine, Thank

Lesson 11
I.   1. order   2. ready   3. take   4. closed
      5. but   6. close   7. front   8. get

II.   help, get, morning, call, room, at, problem

Lesson 12
I.   1. much   2. many   3. are   4. is
      5. high   6. something   7. change   8. take

II.   much, costs, cheaper, price, buy, Here, for

Lesson 13
I.   1. for   2. book   3. take   4. like
      5. anything   6. about   7. to   8. nothing

II.   order, would, rare, drink, have, dessert, menu

Lesson 14

I. 1. pair   2. clothes   3. cloth   4. look
    5. size   6. try   7. brand   8. for

II. take, sale, try, size, much, only, take, Here

Lesson 15

I. 1. hand   2. favor   3. as   4. sounds
    5. madam   6. in   7. corner   8. measurements

II. help, looking, size, so, take, idea, over

Lesson 16

I. 1. size   2. pair   3. Wow   4. shame
    5. ones   6. fit   7. that   8. one

II. fit, size, try, How, afraid, ones, way

Lesson 17

I. 1. of   2. but   3. gone   4. next
    5. consult   6. more   7. smaller   8. look

II. dictionary, one, the, better, expensive, latest, take

Lesson 18

I. 1. by   2. foot   3. take   4. owes
    5. speed   6. keep   7. one   8. in

II. foot, take, by, on, miss, There

Lesson 19

I. 1. booked   2. make   3. stay   4. lived
    5. rates   6. rate   7. See   8. then

II. available, book, reservation, rates, reserve, many, dollars

Lesson 20

I. 1. check   2. have   3. by   4. are
    5. shall   6. will   7. doesn't   8. piece

II. passport, Here, don't, right, charge, accept, fill

Lesson 21

I. 1. do   2. change   3. cash   4. identity
    5. for   6. between   7. How   8. rest

II. cash, identification, card, do, currency, rest, fine

Lesson 22

I. 1. wish   2. birth   3. departs   4. on
    5. at   6. book   7. birthday   8. reconfirm

II. reconfirm, class, economy, flight, on, at, departs

Lesson 23

I. 1. at   2. right   3. go   4. seat
    5. in   6. pieces   7. First   8. for

II. have, first, window, section, luggage, over

Lesson 24

I. 1. out   2. to   3. that   4. must
    5. has   6. see   7. all   8. bad

II. scale, charge, that, see, claim, pass, through, flight

Lesson 25

I. 1. please   2. special   3. mail   4. for
    5. cheaper   6. Though   7. Because   8. but

II. by, weigh, How, register, cheaper, though, That

Lesson 26

I. 1. the   2. a   3. eats   4. have
    5. quite   6. get   7. worried   8. done

II. shot, worried, hurt, over, take, quite, times

Lesson 27

I. 1. ready   2. isn't   3. can't   4. don't
    5. shall   6. will   7. worse   8. take

II. species, sure, aren't, Poor, behaves, shall, ready

Lesson 28

I. 1. take   2. out   3. back   4. full
    5. did   6. if   7. like   8. caught

II. going, at, went, see, took, say, show

Lesson 29

I. 1. quit   2. give   3. future   4. occasion
    5. on   6. fortune   7. like   8. annual

II. experience, willing, overtime, vacation, depends, sound

Lesson 30

I. 1. emergency   2. away   3. on   4. into
    5. ran   6. burned   7. fire   8. Be

II. quick(ly), matter, calling, on, right

英式 IPA 音标与美式 K.K. 音标对照表

序号	IPA	K.K.	Key Words
1	ɪ	ɪ	bit
2	e	ɛ	bed
3	æ	æ	cat
4	ɒ	ɑ	hot
5	ʌ	ʌ	cut
6	ʊ	ʊ	put
7	ə	ə	about
8	i	ɪ	happy
9	u	ʊ	actuality
10	iː	i	bee
11	ɑː	ɑ	father
12	ɔː	ɔ	law
13	uː	u	tool
14	ɜː	ɝ	bird
15	eɪ	e	name
16	aɪ	aɪ	lie
17	ɔɪ	ɔɪ	boy
18	əʊ	o	no
19	aʊ	aʊ	out
20	ɪə	ɪr	beer
21	eə	ɛr	hair
22	ʊə	ʊr	tour
23	uə	ʊə	actual
24	iə	jɚ	peculiar

Notes:

1. K.K.音标取自美国两位语言学家 John S. Kenyon 和 Thomas A. Knott 两人姓氏的第一个字母。其特点是按照一般的美国读法标音。

2. 本列表所用的 IPA 音标是英国 Jones 音标的最新修订形式。

3. K.K.音标除辅音中[ŋ]、[l]与IPA音标[n]、[l]符号不同外，其余基本一致。

4. 美式和英式发音的不同点之一是卷舌音。如果单词的字母组合含有 r，该组合一般会发卷舌音。例：four [fɔː]（IPA）；[fɔr]（K.K.）。